Local Humor

Hugh Gilmore
Janet Gilmore
Jim Harris
Mike Todd

iUniverse, Inc.
New York   Bloomington

Local Humor

iUniverse books may be ordered through booksellers or by contacting:

iUniverse
1663 Liberty Drive
Bloomington, IN 47403
www.iuniverse.com
1-800-Authors (1-800-288-4677)

Because of the dynamic nature of the Internet, any Web addresses or links contained in this book may have changed since publication and may no longer be valid.

Front cover illustration and back cover photograph by Z. Schulz

ISBN: 978-1-4401-4861-3 (pbk)
ISBN: 978-1-4401-4862-0 (ebk)

Printed in the United States of America

iUniverse rev. date: 6/19/2009

Contents

The Loneliness of the Long-Distance Reader 1

Sins of the Flesh 4

Diary 6

Nothing to Fear but the Ferret Itself 10

Me and Mrs. Jones, We Got a Thing Goin' On 12

City Hall 16

Dylan, Suze, Sneezy, Woodstock, Bowling and Me 18

Going Topless 20

Trying to Pry the Remote Control from Melissa Dribben's Hands. .22

Valentine's Day 25

First Fire Drill: Burning Memories 28

The Scrapple Experience 33

Television is a Talking Dog 35

To the New College Graduates 39

Penny Rebellion 42

You've Lost a Friend in Pennsylvania 48

Writing the Soft-Boiled Crime Novel 50

Jobs for Dead People 53

Just Wishin' and Hopin' and Thinkin' and Dreamin',
    Plannin' and Bowlin'. 55

The Corniest Controversy of All 58

Television In Waiting Rooms 60

The Sidewalks of Philadelphia 65

Dinner 67

Finally Passing the Pregnancy Test 69

A Knuckle Sandwich from Robert Mitchum 71

Stuff . . . . Stuff 73

Fever in the Mornin', Fever All through the Night 76

Being Pregnant is Not for the Faint of Stomach 79

Honk If You Hate Noise Pollution 81

Red Tape 85

Fontanel Follies of 1958 88

Wren Things Go Awry 91

The Spoiled Little Prince 93

Dating Your Wife .97

Patiocity 99

Will Mike Get Beaten Up for this Column? 102

So Long Chumps, I'm Taking My Nigerian 419 Money and
    Hitting the Road! 104

Dangerous 107

Snow Wash 109

A Requiem for the Varmint 113

Foreword

Perched on the edge of the beautiful Wissahickon Valley, looking down on the rest of Philadelphia, Chestnut Hill is a neighborhood of stone mansions, gingerbread cottages, and tree-lined streets. First settled by German religious sects in the late 1600's, it lies along an old cobblestone road known as Germantown Avenue. When Chestnut Hillers speak of "The Avenue," suffice to say they are NOT talking about 5th Avenue.

It is a neighborhood replete with community organizations, associations, and well–heeled denizens who care passionately about every aspect of their environs — occasionally to the point of very public battles — and their newspaper, the *Chestnut Hill Local,* is no exception.

More than a mere vehicle for advertisements and wedding announcements, the Local reports on people and issues of regional importance, and is no stranger to controversy, both within and outside of the ranks of the paper. In addition, though, and unlike almost any other community newspaper, the Local regularly runs humor columns.

Penned by a homegrown stable of loony literati, with equal measure humor and humanity, these columns keep the locals laughing through hard times, high water, and whatever else rolls down the Avenue — Germantown Avenue, of course.

So welcome to this exclusive club. Now you, too, can share in the hilarity that keeps Hillers quaking with laughter in the Quaker City.

Acknowledgments

I'd like to thank Hugh, Janet, and Mike for agreeing to be part of this momentous anthology. I have long been a fan of their columns, and occasionally even read them.

Thanks too, to Len Lear and Pete Mazzaccaro, the editors at the Chestnut Hill Local, for allowing us the distinct privilege of having our own columns. Long live the Local!

Further thanks to Janet and Hugh for the lovely dinner party and the giant bag of Cheetos.

And a final and special thank you to our readers, without whom we probably would have quit this writing business long ago and done something constructive with our lives.

After all of the cutting, pasting, laughing, crying, and blood-letting involved in the making of this book is said and done, I think we have produced a document that will secure our proper place in the annals of history for all eternity, or at least until the end of time.

JH
Chestnut Hill
June 2009

The Loneliness of the Long-Distance Reader

By Hugh Gilmore

When honeybees come back to the hive they do a waggle dance to tell their hive mates where they've been and whether it's worth going there. And when dogs and cats and monkeys and horses and bears, and … you know, the animals, get together after an absence, they sniff each other's muzzles (etc.) in order to catch up on the latest news.

So it is with humans too, except that we have language to substitute for scratching and sniffing each other. Language allows us to describe more abstract things than what we've been eating or whom we've been hanging around. For example, it makes it possible for us to tell our friends at the dinner table what we've been reading.

If you ever want the feeling of Odd Man Out at the dinner table, however, try mentioning a book you've read that no one else has even heard of. This has happened to me a lot lately. Admittedly, I'd never heard of these books either before I found them, some in a cardboard box, others on a dusty bookshelf.

These were books of the neglected kind, written a while ago and since shelved and ignored. Perhaps justly, perhaps not. I sometimes simply find myself playing Catcher-In-The-Rye to old books in danger of going over the edge of oblivion.

There are thousands of new books published every year and a diminishing number of readers and time for reading. The competition for our attention is fierce; movies and TV and the Internet and iPods are winning the timeshare battle over books.

In the book world, each generation of newborns pushes the old-borns aside, and leaves them languishing and dusty on the world's libraries' shelves.

Waiting for you and me.

I'll not be mysterious here. As part of my quest for karma there are a few places where I pick up unwanted books and give them away to people who might read them. Occasionally, I find a title irresistible

– Dwarf's Blood, for example, a novel from 1941 – and read it. Then comes the hard part: finding someone to talk to about it.

My friends, for example. Intelligent and interesting people. Trouble is, people like to talk about books that are currently in the news, or popular. That's why the first topic at dinner usually is movies. Who's seen what? Everyone can chime in on that topic. Even if no one has seen the movie. Everyone has seen publicity for it, or read a review and can at least say whether or not they want to see it.

I think this is because people crave being part of a shared experience. It seems almost a need.

In mid-August, I tried at five different table gatherings saying, "I've just read a very interesting novel about a man who lived alone in Antarctica, studying the lives and habits of penguins."

Silence.

"It was written in 1965 by a guy who'd actually lived there, studying penguins."

Brief, respectful pause.

Then the conversational channel switched to an Oprah book which one person present had read, but everyone had something to say about.

No one even asked me the book's title, which was the reason I read it: Forbush and the Penguins, by Graham Billings. Just so you know.

I couldn't resist the title and I also wondered, how could someone construct a novel around the premise of a solitary man in Antarctica? It was expectedly tedious in many ways, I must admit, but terrific nonetheless. It was all about…a guy named Forbush…and…penguins. Loveable creatures, those. Oh, and it was action-packed — in a slow, slow way. I really can't recommend it or not recommend it.

Since I read around 100 books a year, an odd book here or there doesn't diminish the year's reading experience for me the way it would if I only read five or ten a year and hit a clunker. All in the day's work, actually. That's how Forbush talked. A New Zealander, actually. It was quite honest about how cruelly nature works, come to think of it. Forbush thought a lot. Though the title sounds whimsical, the book was definitely non-Disney.

And, in for a penny, in for a pound, after Forbush, I decided to intensify my non-relevance as a dinner-table companion by picking up and reading another book whose title intrigued me. That would be

Blind Raftery, by Donn Byrne, better known as the author of Messer Marco Polo. Again, the title pulled me in. Blind Raftery is a famous "dark man," i.e. he's blind, but also a poet, singing bard, wandering minstrel who is walking from Galway to Mayo in Ireland with his wife, Hilaria.

If you need a quick short book for your list, this book is small, brief, and narrow, with about seven words per line. On the other hand, it's written in a slow-to-read Irish dialect, beautifully poetic, and was written with the old-fashioned sentiments typical of its era (1924). But in its own, take-yer-time way, it is gripping, funny, horrible, suspenseful, and touching.

I haven't a clue as to how to mention it at future dinner tables. Should I say, "Good news everyone: I've read Blind Raftery at last"? Or just mention that I've read a book from 1924 about a blind Irish poet/bard? Or just keep it to myself and go see the new Woody Allen movie so I can stimulate a conversation next time I see my friends and family?

Ah well, the loneliness of the reader of the obscure. At the least, by virtue of this monologue I've managed to get two of the world's many neglected authors' names said aloud once again.

There's a kind of resurrection and temporary life in that, isn't there?

Sins of the Flesh

By Jim Harris

As a dedicated follower of fashion, I can report that last summer was the least clothed, most exposed in recent memory, following a disturbing trend of leaving less and less to the imagination that began sometime in the late 1990's.

Yes, I am a prude. Thanks for noticing. Other prudes call me a prude. And yes, I am proud to say that I am ashamed of my body, and not only mine, but yours too. And not only ashamed, but afraid. Sore afraid. I would actually be more comfortable being pure energy than flesh and blood, except that I don't really have that much energy. I guess I'm still trying to figure out who I am. It's a process of elimination. I'm not Hugh Hefner. I'm not the Pope. I'm somewhere in the middle, which is still apparently a good bit to the conservative side of current American mores.

I grew up in the 1960's; free love, skinny-dipping, and the whole nine and a half yards. As a good Catholic boy, I was always a bit uneasy with that aspect of the revolution, but I tried to fit in. Now in my 60's, I have lost all childlike fascination with body parts, and am strongly in favor of clothes. Clothing is the only thing that separates us from the other animals. If animals started wearing clothes tomorrow, in no time they'd have libraries and schools and space programs. Conversely, as humans increasingly divest themselves of clothing, civilization declines. The signs are everywhere:

Peek-a-boo clothing revealing bodies that are waxed, polished, tanned, tucked and tattooed. If you're that in love with yourself, please, get a room.

Studs, rings, brads and tacks over, under, around and through every salient feature of the anatomy. Excuse me; you're frightening the children.

Flip-flops. Is there anyone who hates flip-flops more that I do? I hope so, because this is a huge burden to carry alone. Flip flops are not outerwear. Folks who wear them on the street are too lazy to bend over and put on a shoe. These people should be banished to fenced-in flip-flop colonies in the Amazon. Face it; feet are the gnarled, calloused appendages of gross ambulation, and no matter how you paint them, not objects of art to be shared with the world.

Cleavage? We've got it. Busts have not seen this much daylight since Dolly Parton bent over to pick up a penny. Women and girls of late have been tripping over each other and themselves, trying to push the envelope ever lower in an incomprehensible trend that could only have been instigated by a man.

Speaking of men, how about the young men who walk around with their baggy pants falling down around their hips, and their underwear hanging out? Do the ladies find that attractive? Will these men reproduce? One can only hope. And of course, there's the classic "man-with-tool-belt" traveling peep show. Been there, seen that, still bearing scars.

Even the staid, venerable YMCA apparently thinks it's okay for men to shower in open communal areas like wild monkeys. Personally, I find it just a tad uncomfortable to see the same strangers out in the lobby that I just saw au naturel in the showers. That's not the kind of information that I want occupying space in my brain. Remember, this is not the army; I'm paying to be there. Would a stall with a curtain be too much to expect in the twenty-first century?

Here's the deal folks, don't show me yours and I won't show you mine. You may think that the human body is natural and beautiful and all that jazz, but personally I am about twenty thousand years of evolution beyond that worldview. Maybe if we had nice fur or feathers like some other animals, we could conduct our business in our birthday suits, but we don't, so let's just grow up and accept it. In the words of Richard M. Nixon, a great prude in his own right, "Some things are just better left covered up."

Diary

By Janet Gilmore

30 December

My New Year Resolutions are:

1. To lose weight.
2. To develop some poise and tact.
3. To keep the house cleaner.
4. To grow some tomatoes this summer.

My resolutions are very boring, and I wish I could come up with new ones. If I can't keep the ones I make, I might as well resolve to fly to Jupiter, wear only clothing encrusted with jewels or made of gossamer, or find a plastic surgeon who can make me look 10 years old again.

Hugh resolved to lose weight, exercise and read 100 books in the new year. He also declared this the year of "no shoulds." We'll try to free ourselves of the word "should."

Andrew resolved to try to eat a new food this year. I suggested macaroni and cheese; he said, "No, chocolate syrup."

Hugh said we should consult a nutritionist.

31 December

New Year's Eve. The family celebrated here. We ate chicken and potatoes and watched people on TV singing "If I Could Turn Back Time." Lots of disagreement about exactly how much plastic surgery they've had. "All of it," said one sister. Hugh mentioned in passing that there's a website called celebritynippleslip.com. The man certainly knows his way around the Internet.

We watched a video of *Men in Black*. Not the Will Smith one but the one starring the Three Stooges as surgeons. Every time the Public Address system said, "Paging Dr. Howard, Dr. Fine, Dr. Howard," we all cracked up. We watch it every New Year's Eve.

I called my mother at midnight. She said they had a New Year

6

celebration at Walker City Retirement Home, but the staff set the clocks ahead two hours, as the elderly residents have trouble staying up 'til midnight. They all had a great time counting down to zero at exactly ten seconds [before 10:00?]. I'm not sure exactly how that works.

"Did you know that Dad and I went to Times Square for New Year's Eve once?" Mom said.

"When?" I asked.

"A few years ago. I don't remember if Dad was still alive or not."

Her memory is not what it was.

After everyone left, Hugh, our son Andrew and I sat on the sofa and read last year's calendar/diary. We remembered the things we did. It seemed like a lot for a family that doesn't go anywhere or do anything. We we're surprised every year when we see the number of ticket stubs and programs and photographs in our book. We had some fun, and nobody in the family died. We count it as a good year. We drank one last toast to ourselves, kissed goodnight and went to bed.

1 January

New Year's Day. We got up at the crack of noon.

I don't like national holidays very much. Everything is closed and there's nowhere to go.

I made oatmeal for breakfast as a tribute to our new healthy lifestyle. Andrew wouldn't try it. He said he wasn't hungry, and went up to his room.

Later, I reminded him to brush his teeth.

"I'm not a baby — you don't have to remind me," he said.

I noticed on every trip to the bathroom, however, that his toothbrush was still dry and the toothpaste was still capped.

"Andrew, brush your teeth."

"I did."

"No, you didn't."

"Yes, I did!"

"No, you didn't."

"How do you know?"

"Because I'm your mother." I didn't want to tell him how I knew, because if I told, he'd simply wet the toothbrush and uncap the toothpaste, and *still* not brush his little fangs.

"No, really, how do you know?"

Luckily, he heard the theme music of a TV show that he wanted to see, so I was off the hook for the moment.

Hugh bundled up and went for a speed walk at the local school track. I did a step aerobics video workout in the basement, and managed to sweat.

Hugh gave me a book of love sonnets for Christmas. I found it on my night table tonight.

"Why is this here?" I asked.

"So I can read you one sonnet every night."

"I thought you meant me to read one to myself every night. That would be very boring. I didn't know you were going to read them to me."

"That was my intent."

He read a sonnet by Dante, I guess to Beatrice. It was nice.

2 January

When I brought clean laundry up to Andrew's room, I smelled something too good to be a young boy's natural odor. I followed my nose to the baseboard heater, where Andrew had hidden what's left of his Christmas candy, which had melted in its foil wrappers into a Dali-esque Santa Claus, some swooning snowmen and a few soft bells. I removed all I could find. No wonder he's never hungry at mealtimes. He also tucked several used Kleenex and a few small toys in the heater as well. Must discuss the nature of fire with him. And the importance of roughage in the diet.

Stores re-opened. We bought a new scale to record our weight loss in the new year. A Health-o-Meter. It's digital and measures in half-pound increments. It can read your weight in metric system, too, but who cares?

I also bought a "Down Replacement" pillow for Hugh. Not sure what "down replacement" means – I think it might be "up," but what does *that* mean? What is an "up" pillow? Sounds like something that promotes insomnia. We'll see.

At bedtime, Hugh read me Sonnet #2 by Petrarch. It made no sense to either of us. We agreed that it lost everything in translation.

I lay in bed tonight, looking at nothing in particular.

HUGH: Why aren't you reading?

ME: I'm thinking.

HUGH: Well, don't – it leads nowhere and you make me nervous. Pretend you're reading.

3 January

I returned the new pillow. Hugh didn't like it. He suggested I tell the customer service clerk, "My husband swore he felt a pea under it," but I didn't have the nerve. I didn't really need a reason. The clerk asked me if I'd like to choose another pillow, but I didn't know how to replace "Down Replacement," and I was sure she didn't know, either.

Nothing to Fear but the Ferret Itself

By Mike Todd

For the record, I was originally going to the pet store to buy fish. They had these cute green puffer fish that cruised around the tank like fat little swimming Legos. Of course, the puffers were saltwater fish, which means that, had I taken them home, they would have been dead in three minutes. That would have been a double tragedy, because not only would I have killed innocent fish, but I'm also a terrible cook. I have no idea what you'd even put on puffer fish. Saucony peppers? See, that's not even a real kind of pepper. It's a running shoe. Good thing I didn't get the fish.

As I stood at the fish tank in the store, picking out which puffers I'd like to take home with me, my wife Kara wandered over to the "small animal" section of the store, where people pay good money to bring home the kinds of animals that other people pay good money for the Orkin man to remove.

Four hours later, I pushed an overflowing shopping cart out of the store, and Kara had a baby ferret curled up in the pocket of her sweater. We named him Chopper, after the junkyard dog in the best movie ever made, "Stand by Me," though we have yet to teach him the signature trick of his namesake (if you are unfamiliar with the film, I can only offer my condolences).

Once we got back to our place, I began piecing the wire siding and plastic brackets of the dumpster-sized cage together. I looked down at my new little friend, who looked back up at me, scared and curious. His furry little weasel life was in our hands, and we were all beginning to understand that. I'd never been responsible for the life of another creature before. At that moment, I was honestly moved, and then so were his bowels.

"Hey, he just went on the carpet!" I said.

"Get his cage together! You need him in the cage to start litter training him," Kara said, fresh from Googling "litter train ferret."

Chopper wandered around the room, checked out every corner, then looked back at us and fertilized the carpet again.

"He did it again!" I said. "How is that possible?"

"Hurry! We need the cage!" Kara said.

Half an hour later, as I was squeezing the last little plastic bracket onto the cage, sweat dripping from my nose, we breathed a sigh of relief. The nightmare was over. And as I went to pick up our little varmint to introduce him to his new home, he did his business on the carpet again.

"What have we done? Oh, what have we done?" I said. "Did we keep the receipt?"

That day was almost four years ago, and Chopper hasn't been out of his cage since. That's a joke. Occasionally, we let him have conjugal visits with squirrels in the front yard. Actually, he's earned free run of the house. He spends most of his time with his head in people's shoes, or rummaging through my backpack looking for granola bars.

He loves the granola bars. Ferrets are apparently carnivores in the wild, but Chopper won't even look at meat. He wants raisins, peanut butter, and granola bars. His tastes aren't actually all that discerning, as he also tries to eat soap, paint and feminine hygiene products, but I still respect his decision to be a vegetarian.

We didn't realize when we bought Chopper that we were getting a hippie ferret. Once, when he got out of the house by ripping a hole in the screen door, we found him three days later in the parking lot outside of an Allman Brothers concert, selling hummus and brownies out of the back of a Volkswagen van. I'm still trying to brush the flowers out of his hair.

You can send Chopper's backstage pass to Mike Todd at mikectodd@gmail.com.

Me and Mrs. Jones, We Got a Thing Goin' On

By Hugh Gilmore

I'm surprised this doesn't happen to me more often, writing for the Local so regularly, but you know: you build up a following and then the stalking starts. Women! Where were they when I was sixteen and needed them?

This latest threat to my happy marriage began innocently enough with an email one morning from one of my out-of-town readers. Here's part of the message:

Good Day Dear.

How is your day?

my name is miss Ruth martin am 24yrs old girl Single ,
My dear am in search of some one who will understand
life as love as trust b ecause i need true love beleive me,
well i just fill like to say hi to prove my intrest to you .
please awaiting to hear from you, kisses with love
Miss Ruth

Holy cow! I thought. They say you're not supposed to write back when you get e-mails like this, but I was sure this wasn't random. I'd written what I thought was a great column the day before and this was the inevitable result. Groupies. I wrote back, hoping to nip this in the bud.

Dear Miss Ruth,

Please understand me and believe me, I am happily married to this day. My wife thinks you love me and I do not even know you, so please stop this chatter with me.

Fondly, regretfully, Hugh

Ruth wrote back the next day:

Good Day My Dearest Love,

Firstly I thank you for your response to my email ... after viewing your profile, I have been obliged to lay a more trust on you due to my situation here in the refugee camp in Dakar Senegal.

Let me first of all reveal my self to you ... I will really like us to have a good relationship in spite of anything because I have this feeling that you are mine .

So, i decided to run away to where i am now. I wish to contact you personally for a long-term relationship that may lead us to somewhere better if we work well on it.

My father of blessed memory deposited the sum of (US$3, 700, 000.00) (three Million Seven Hundred Thousand Dollars) in one of the leading Banks in EUROPE with my name as the next of kin. Could you assist me for the transfer and investment of the fund. I will like to complete my studies under you

You will arrange for my trip to join you over there in your country for us to share this feelings face to face. I was told that this will involve some money for charges.

Yours forever, Ruth

I tried to stop the obviously building momentum:

And good day to you Ruth,

But please, we do not have a personal relationship, so how can you call me "My Dearest Love"?

Don't you think that's superficial?

Love takes time to grow. The picture of me that accompanies my column was taken a full two years ago.

Also, I told you that we cannot have a personal relationship. My wife has threatened to hit me with a rolling pin, which is a thing we use to make pies with in this country if you keep writing to me.

And that cannot happen between you and me because my wife looks over my shoulder when I read my mail. Please give up your devoted interest in me. I would like to have a no-night stand with you.

Regrets, as always, Hugh

Not to be deterred, Ruth replied:

Good Day Dearest One,

I thank you ones again . I will also like to see you face to face ... I know you are the man am going to spend the rest of my life with. I am not going to give your love to any other man you will satisfy me, so needless of looking for another man. Please i have not told anyone except you about the existence of this money and i will like you to please keep it secret to other people because since it is (MONEY) all eyes will be on it.

My love is for you and you alone ... I have informed the bank about my plans to claim this money and the only thing they told me is to look for a foreign partner who will stand on my behalf due to my refugee status and the laws of this country. You will have 15% of the total money helping me and the remaining money will be managed by you in any business of your choice ... Also, 5% for any expenses that might come up in this transfer.

i promise to be kind and will equally need you in every area of my life plus investing ...

i remain your love for ever my love i am in love with you

Miss Ruth Martin.

Well, a columnist gets fan mail once in a while, but this was something else. I replied:

Dear Ruth,

You are a persistent little woman, I'll give you that, but I am telling you that you are making my wife jealous. Now she does not trust me to go to our American game of bowling on League nights, which are Wednesdays. Instead I had to stay home and help her shake out the sheets and wash dishes while my men friends were having fun. She thought I wanted to meet you. Perhaps I should not have dabbed cologne on my wrists, but I thought it would improve my grip since I sweat profusely there.

Please. This is no joke, Ruth. Please stop committing yourself to me and the idea of a lifetime of happiness with me that is impossible. I would rather stay in my little frying pan than leap out, if you know what I mean.

So please, Ruth, get over your silly infatuation with me.

In closing I will say that though I have never seen a photo of you I find your skill at handling large numbers of money and international finance quite attractive. It is a skill I have always wished my wife would acquire.

Oh well, as St Thomas, the saint, once said, "Pray that you do not fall into the hands of woman who counts cards at Blackjack." I have added that prayer to my rosary. It took one hour exactly to add the extra bead, as the links are quite small on my rosary.

I'll close by saying Stop reading my Local column if you can't stand the heat. Yours (not!), Hugh

I think that did it. She stopped writing, but for about a week after that I received fifteen e-mails a day telling me " Hello friend ! You have just received a postcard Greeting from someone who cares about you..."

I haven't opened any of them yet. I'm considering a pseudonym.

(PS: The above letters have been condensed from actual correspondence. I do not recommend what I did in replying to "Ruth Martin.")

City Hall

By Jim Harris

I recently received a delinquent tax bill from the city. No explanation, just "Tax Due, Interest, Penalty - Pay Immediately." I knew it was wrong. I knew I couldn't possibly owe them that much money, but I also knew that it would cost me precious time and energy to straighten it out. And why did it take eight months of accruing interest and penalties for them to notify me? With trembling hands, I stuffed the letter into my fax machine and sent it off packing to my tax lady.

A word of advice; unless you're a cave-dwelling hermit who survives solely on twigs and berries, you need a professional tax person. Someone like the "Rain Man," who can count falling snowflakes and know intuitively that Flag Day 1969 was a sunny Tuesday. Otherwise, you're doomed to spend your productive life running through a maze called City Hall.

So my tax lady said she'd phone the revenue department, but that it would be helpful if I gathered up my papers, marched down to City Hall and found the right person with whom to speak. My heart sank.

What the average citizen might not know is that the city doesn't WANT you to find the right person, and if you do, they don't want you to be able to understand them. I have often thought that the people who do the absolute worst on the city job applications are the very ones assigned to be gatekeepers at the portals of information.

Of course, in reality, no one ever actually "applies" for a city job - positions are "bestowed" according to ancient traditions of cronyism and nepotism that date all the way back to Pennsylvania's Quaker roots. That's the American way — any girl, boy or potted plant can grow up to be a well-paid bumbling bureaucrat. It's all in the timing. When a robot is elected mayor, important city jobs will go to robots. Personally, I can hardly wait.

After arranging time off from work and paying twenty dollars to park, I walked in to City Hall and asked where I could find the revenue department. The woman at the information desk interrupted her conversation with another "at-large" city worker just long enough to say, "Banama glomma," and limply gesture in the general direction of nothing in particular.

Forthwith, I embarked upon the nebulous course given me, then noticed the words "Revenue Department" in four-foot high letters on a wall in the exact opposite direction. I followed an arrow and wandered through a labyrinth of nondescript hallways, doors and stairs until I eventually found myself back at the information desk. The previous woman was apparently on a break, as there was now a very large man sound asleep behind the counter.

Afraid to awaken him, I opted to return to the labyrinth, and this time, by following the sounds of dull moaning, found the cavernous waiting room. There were no clear lines or systems of any kind in effect, only a sprawling gray sea of hopeless humanity. The scene resembled one of those pitiful refugee camps you see on the nightly news. Off in the distance, I could see three cubicles that apparently held the besieged disbursers of official mumbo-jumbo, but there didn't appear to be any movement of people in their direction.

The only time the crowd shrunk in size was when someone committed suicide, starved to death, or was eaten by a marauding band of zombies. I sat on the floor to wait, and after reading Bill Clinton's autobiography — twice — decided that I'd rather live my life as an outlaw than die here in the tomb of the unknown taxpayer. I ran home and started packing my bags.

I planned to hide out in the swamps behind the oil refineries, where even the Parking Authority could never find me. My packing was interrupted by a phone call from my tax lady. She said that she had finally gotten through to a real person on the phone, and not only did I NOT owe the city money, but I had a refund due. Unfortunately, I could not receive the refund because, they claimed, I had not filed a tax return for 1996, a year for which I no longer have any records. They suggested that I get in touch with the IRS and try to find my "Schedule C" for that year.

I think I'm just gonna go ahead and live in the swamps. It's much easier to deal with snakes and leeches than City Hall.

Dylan, Suze, Sneezy, Woodstock, Bowling and Me

By Janet Gilmore

NEWS ITEM: *August 15 is the anniversary of the Woodstock concert at Saugerties, N.Y. Many former kids, then enjoying illegal drugs, nowadays on prescription drugs, planned to re-unite, but their plan was cancelled.*

Oh, man! Suze Rotolo just wrote a book: *A Freewheelin' Time: A Memoir of Greenwich Village.* Just in case you were cryogenically frozen or unborn during the 1960-70's, and don't know, Suze Rotolo is the girl in the snow, clinging to Bob Dylan on the cover of his *Freewheelin' Bob Dylan* album. Her book describes being with Bob Dylan at the beginning of his career and how his fame affected them both.

I was right there at the time. I went to N.Y.U. in Greenwich Village. Bob never met me, though, so after all, I had to come back to Philadelphia and hang out with myself.

Under a lot of parental pressure to stop wasting time and SETTLE DOWN, I got a job and sought a husband. If I had actually met a folk singer at a party, say, I'd have been intrigued. Given a propensity to waste myself on jerks, I probably would have fallen in love.

ME: Dad, I met a great guy!

DAD: What does he do?

ME: He's a folk singer!

DAD: A folk singer?

ME: Yup - cool, huh?

DAD: From *this* he makes a living?

I needed more information about my future than Bob Dylan could offer at the beginning of his career.

Looking at the review of Rotolo's book, though, made me kind of nostalgic for the 60-70's. And jealous of her freedom. Me, I had to earn a livin', though I wasn't near willin', crazy job was a villain, no tokin' nor swillin', with Suze and Bob Dylan!

After all, that could have been ME on that album cover — Bob Dylan's girlfriend —even though, okay, Suze has perfect hair.

Every jingle-jangle mornin' for years, I got up when the alarm went off, got dressed and went out the door to teach junior high school. I could have hung with Bob and Suze in the studio instead of in the classroom. I could have been pub-crawling somewhere cool instead of crawling hopelessly to locker inspection and lunchroom duty.

That album cover tears at me. There's Dylan, walking in the snow in New York City, a cute girl on his arm (neither of them dressed warmly enough, I now notice), likely going to get coffee or a meal after Bob just recorded *Blowin' in the Wind* or some other genius song. Then they went back to their warm pad in the East Village to watch the snow fall, and get it on. Listen to some music. I bet they didn't set the alarm clock for the next morning.

My own boyfriend at that time, Sneezy, the dwarf of Snow White's seven he most closely resembled, told me he lived in a pad in New York (turned out to be Yonkers, with his parents), was not a folk singer, but an engineer who became a teacher to avoid the Vietnam draft, and had not an atom of poetry in his soul. A simple question and answer put him out of my heart forever, even though my parents liked him.

(*Summer 1969*)

> ME: Hey, Sneezy, there's a free rock concert upstate all weekend - wanna go?
> SNEEZY: Forget it — we'll never get a parking spot.

True story. That's the reason I missed Woodstock. And Dylan. And Suze Rotolo got to be the girl on the album cover. And have a life worthy of a book. And poor me. I had to stay in Philadelphia, get married, have a fine son, and settle for happiness.

Janet Gilmore is still hanging out in Philadelphia. In nice weather, her family's laundry can be seen blowin' in the wind. Peace and love.

Going Topless

By Mike Todd

My wife Kara and I just stared at our jeep sitting in the driveway, naked. I mean the jeep was sitting in the driveway naked, not us, though we had been stripped of some of our security.

"You definitely didn't take the top down last night?" she asked.

"Nope. I sure didn't," I said.

It was a Thursday morning about a year ago, and we had just discovered that the soft top had been stolen off our jeep, which was parked right in front of our house, during the night. The year before that, at our old apartment complex, the stereo head unit had been yanked out of the dashboard, leaving a gaping hole, a tangle of hastily cut wires and my desire to reinstate Hammurabi's Code.

Leaving a jeep with a soft top unattended overnight is like parking a giant Twinkie next to an elementary school playground, expecting it to still be there when you return. (Kids these days still eat Twinkies, don't they? From the looks of 'em, I'm going to guess yes.) There's just no good way to secure a jeep, other than parking it inside a bigger car made of metal and glass, or perhaps inside a garage, but who can actually fit a car in the garage with all those old tennis balls and rusty bikes in the way?

We had been toying with the idea of selling the jeep anyway – jeeps somehow manage to combine the fuel efficiency of an Abrams tank with the carrying capacity of a newborn burro – and having the roof stolen was the last straw. We replaced the soft top and sold the jeep two weeks later.

This whole episode was just a distant, expensive memory until last week, when the detective called. They caught the guy stealing something else, and for some reason (hopefully extreme duress), he admitted to stealing our jeep top, too. The detective asked me if I wanted him to arrest the guy, which should have been the easiest question I've ever been asked, but then I started thinking about how maybe the guy needed our jeep top to build a crude shelter for his family, or how maybe he had to cut it into small pieces and sauté it in rainwater just to feed his children one more meal.

Just kidding. "Yes! Please, arrest him," I said. "If you could taser him, too, that would be cool."

The detective brought a deposition over to our house, which gave me the rare opportunity to sign an official police document other than a speeding ticket. The detective scored extra points for not reacting even the slightest bit as our ferret crawled over his shoes and into the folds of his overcoat. These guys must go through some intense anti-flinching training.

The next step now is for me and Kara to meet with the assistant district attorney, which I'm really excited about, because if there's anything I've learned from watching Law and Order reruns every night for the past four years, it's that assistant district attorneys are really, really hot. Also, different hot women rotate into the position every couple of seasons. By the time they get promoted to regular old district attorneys, though, they turn into craggy old men.

The long and short of it is that we'll probably get the old jeep top back, which works out just perfectly for us, because we sold the jeep last year. Wait, no, that's not perfect at all. What are we going to do with a beat-up old jeep top? I can already feel the pack rat genes my Dad gave me stirring deep in my soul, saying, "Put it in the garage. You never know when you might need it."

You can share your Twinkie with Mike Todd at mikectodd@gmail.com.

Trying to Pry the Remote Control
from Melissa Dribben's Hands

By Hugh Gilmore

*"I saw the best minds of my generation destroyed by
madness, starving hysterical naked ... looking for an angry fix ..."*

(From Allen Ginsberg's *HOWL*, 1957)

Will anyone join me in a worried-villagers' midnight parade — you
know: torches, pitchforks, the works — demanding the safe return of
Melissa Dribben's mind? We could even ask the local schools to offer
community service credits to students who don't have a cause yet.
Perhaps some local tavern could stage a benefit and we could arrange
to have poor Melissa treated.

It's the least we could do. For years Melissa has been one of our
town's treasured assets. A great person, a gifted mind, and an intrepid
reporter for the *Philadelphia Inquirer* (one of our local newspapers, sort
of a *City Paper* that doesn't take risqué ads yet). Her feature stories over
the years have entertained, inspired, and moved us. Her work ethic,
her sense of humor, and her honesty have made her writing a pleasure
to read.

Unfortunately, that same honesty she is noted for, now reveals she
has gone 'round the bend and is in danger of never coming back. If
you follow her columns faithfully, as I do, you know what I'm talking
about.

On February 22, Melissa publicly declared her mental emancipation
when she described how she allowed Cable TV into her house for the
first time. Until then, Melissa, as a parent, had created an idyllic home
atmosphere by encouraging her children to read, and play mentally
challenging games, and listen to music. She did not want their minds
polluted or warped by the insidious, false, materialistic values promoted

by American commercial television. Their TV set was primitive at best. Time spent watching TV was severely regulated. This atmosphere was difficult to maintain, but worth the effort.

Her declaration column carried the following headline:

Confessions of an addict: A power higher than any couch potato has mandated the switch to digital TV. The time has come to give in.

What followed was a passage equal in horror and desperation to Bronte's description of Mister Rochester's mad wife in *Jane Eyre*. You know, the hidden loony, the "dark secret" of the family, sitting in the gloomy attic, all hope gone.

It seems that, following the federal mandate to switch from analog to digital TV, Melissa was enticed to get Cable TV with some "On Demand" options. The addiction began almost immediately.

Every night, she says. She scrambles into bed to do this. She ignores her daughter's pleas to play Scrabble in order to fill in "every millisecond" of her life with "passive, mind-rotting entertainment." In typical addict terms, she related, "... what a sweet rush it's been ... a delicious thrill ... hour upon hour" of watching shows like *Monk*.

Her children, she says, are appalled and tell her it's a sickness. She admits it, but doesn't care. The fault, she says, lies in the fact that her own parents let her watch all the TV she wanted when she was a child. Now she has atavistically become her former self. As the twig is bent, the tree is inclined.

We're left to wonder, what's next: TV dinners? Streamed sitcoms on her iPod? An inability to dine out at places that don't have a TV at the bar?

There's no telling, but for now we must leave her, sitting upstairs in the bedroom, possibly howling with delight, as hour after hour of the cold blue light washes over her. Try to say a prayer for her, will you, if you walk by during our candlelight vigil outside her house. We're not sure which house it is. It's somewhere in Chestnut Hill and I'm told you can spot it by looking for the cool eerie rays of a television set glowing through one of the upstairs windows. Can't be too many houses like that in the neighborhood, I'd think.

In the meantime, some of the rest of you are going to have to help me pick up the "Enemies of the Enemies of Reading" slack created by Melissa's recent passing to the other side. We're going to have to redistribute the workload.

And let this be a lesson to the rest of you in the Fahrenheit 451 club: TV = Bad. Cable TV= Worse. Almost everyone who has ever subscribed to cable TV has become overwhelmed by the false sense of bounty it stimulates with its hundreds of channels. Some people recover within a few months, rediscovering their ability to smell elephant doo in their homes. Others remain anosmic for life.

We live in dim dumb times. Our community needs her sharp mind more than ever. Please join me in wishing Melissa a speedy recovery.

Valentine's Day

When it comes to bandying, no word is more bandied about than "love," and love's big day is, of course, Valentine's Day. A little history is in order. Saint Valentine may or may not have been a martyr of ancient Rome. His birth date and birthplace are unknown, and nothing is known about his life. He was de-sainted in 1969. So much for the origins of the holiday.

Everyone knows that the real icon of Valentine's Day is Cupid, the Roman god who determines our fate in matters of love. And really, who better equipped for such an important job than a naked, flying baby? Sometimes he is depicted as wearing a diaper, which actually isn't a bad idea for a flying baby.

Valentine's Day is also known as Male Guilt Day, since it is the day when all men are required to atone for their colossal unworthiness by presenting their partners with fancy, frilly items. Leading up to V-day, stores that sell things like potpourri and teddy bears are suddenly full of gruff, burly men looking like deer caught in the headlights as they clutch ornate cards with headings like "To my Dear Precious Darling Wife," or "Our Love is Like an Artichoke." A few men always panic and run out the door, but driven ever onward by primeval forces, most do complete the quest.

As difficult and painful as that quest is, Valentine's Day is even rougher on those fellows who have no mates. I'm talking about the poor shlubs who haven't bought any new clothes or cleaned their apartments in 20 years, which was probably the last time they had a date. As someone who has spent almost 30 years of his adult life as a bachelor, I have a few dubious tips to share with my lonesome brethren.

If you place a personal ad, mention that you like polka dots, rainbows, and walking in the rain. Try to use the phrase "God-fearing" in a sentence. Don't mention kickboxing or dentures. Don't say that you are an astronaut or a CIA agent unless it is true. Trust me, lies like that will come back to haunt you, and you could wind up as the subject of an eyewitness news undercover investigation.

Don't look for soul mates at the car-vacuuming place. Anyone who is that neat will vacuum you out of her life and deposit you in the dust bin of history before you've even had time to sit down.

Elevators in office buildings are good places to meet women. Once you get past security, you can ride up and down all day if you like. Wear a suit and pretend to talk about stock trading on your fake cell phone. Whenever possible, surreptitiously slip your business cards into women's tote bags. If they do phone you, you'll have about two minutes to win them over before they decide to call the police.

Here are several different types of pickup lines. Use them sparingly.

Cute: "I'm sorry, but I HAD to stare at your chest. It's in my 'Contract with America'."

Impressive: "I have a five-foot-long colon!"

Intellectual: "You know, I often reflect upon myself reflecting upon myself."

Blunt: "I missed The Love Train, now I'm just waiting for The Sex Train."

When preparing for a date, don't fuss too much over your hair. It's bad if your hair looks better than the rest of you, but if your hair should spring a "wing," cut the wing off. That will remove the offending hairs as well as discourage other hairs that might be contemplating similar behavior.

For God's sake, if you're an older guy with gray hair, don't dye it jet-black unless you want to look like your face is being sucked into a black hole. If you have already dyed it, just say that you're starring in "The Roy Orbison Story" in community theater. Do not, under any circumstance, wax your mustache. Sporting this look is like having the words, "I have taken a vow of celibacy" tattooed on your face. You might as well go ahead and chew tobacco, too, because you're not going to be doing any dating.

When dining out, avoid mustard. It will find its way onto your clothes like squirrels onto a bird feeder. Don't eat so much that you have to loosen your clothing, and don't get drunk. If you wear glasses, make sure they fit properly. Glasses that fly off your face every time you turn your head can be a turnoff.

If your conversational tone is more like Curly of the Three Stooges than Barry White, then get yourself a book of sexy quotations and practice saying them in a non stooge-like manner. For example, lower your voice about two octaves and say, "You know Baby, love is like an artichoke." Allow for a lustful, pregnant pause afterwards while you stare deeply into her eyes.

In the future, you may be able to have yourself cloned and marry the clone. Then, if it doesn't work out, you'll only have yourself to blame. Until that time, however, we'll all just have to look for mates in other, non-cloned human beings, and blame *them* when things don't work out. Heads up. Here comes Cupid.

First Fire Drill: Burning Memories

By Janet Gilmore

Ted, the old shop teacher was retiring from Cedarbrook Middle School at the end of the school year. Thank goodness. He weighed three hundred pounds, had a voice to match his heft and used his voice mostly to embarrass young teachers. I was one of those young teachers at the time.

Ted wore a crew-cut all through the sixties and seventies, just to protest what was going on around him. The first time I went into his wood shop, I asked meekly if I could have a little nail to hang up a little picture of the Eiffel Tower in my classroom.

"NAIL?" he boomed, his voice rising above the machinery,

"WE DON'T HAVE NAILS HERE, JANNIE — WE GLUE AND WE SCREW!" I took him at his word until he started to laugh.

Kids stopped working and looked hopefully at their friends when they thought they heard the word "screw" - they always do. I was so embarrassed, I held my lesson plan book over my face and tried to leave the shop without walking into some power tool and being ground up into tiny pieces, and I never went back.

But there we sat in the teachers' lounge at the end of Ted's last year, telling funny stories about teaching.

"You know, Jannie, one of the funniest things I ever saw was your first fire drill when you were new around here," yelled Ted. I knew exactly what he meant and we shared a genuine laugh for the first and only time.

I taught Junior High French on the theory that while I was waiting with the patience of a saint for my dream job and/or very rich husband to appear, I might as well earn a living so I could better myself and order things from catalogues. The thrill of a paycheck kept me in place for twenty-eight more years.

The troubles started right away at my first fire drill as a brand new teacher. The school told the teachers when the first fire drill was scheduled – it was not meant to be a surprise. So I had had a week or two to prepare.

The fire bell rang in my study hall classroom on a beautiful September day. There I was, 22 years old, and in charge of something for the first time in my life. I remembered from my own school days, that the normal procedure during a fire drill was to find my friends, see if anyone had candy, then catch up on the latest gossip as we sauntered from the building, so blithe were we, but I suspected that wasn't how things worked if you were a teacher, which I now was. I quickly read the faded directions hanging on the bulletin board in my room.

"Okay, boys and girls," I said, "leave the classroom, turn left and go outside quickly and quietly." The fire bell continued to clang. It was LOUD! My students saw my lips moving, but couldn't hear what I was saying.

"WHAT?!" they yelled.

"...QUICKLY AND QUIETLY!" I screamed and pointed.

Luckily my classroom was right next to the exit. It was amazing — the kids looked around to find their friends, asked if anyone had any candy, and tried to catch up on the latest gossip, but basically they did what I told them to do. They filed out silently to the accompaniment of lots of teachers and administrators in the hall, all yelling,

"I said QUIET!"

"NO talking during a Fire Drill!"

"Kids, stay in a straight line!"

"If this was a real fire," added Mr. Doofus, the assistant principal, completely ignoring the needed subjunctive tense, "you'd need to hear emergency directions!"

"Miss Goodman, keep your class in order!"

"Beth," I said, passing the baton of blame off to the nearest student, "Stop talking! Report to the office!"

"Miss Goodman, I told you yesterday, I changed my name to Starshine! Don't call me Beth!" said Beth. It was 1969.

"Fine, okay, Starshine, report to the office!" Starshine did an abrupt turnaround and started for the office.

"Now? During the fire?" she queried over her shoulder.

"No, not now..."

"But you said report to the office..."

"When the fire drill is over!"

"You did tell her to go the office," said several of her helpful little friends. "So, like, if she burns to death, it's your fault, Miss Goodman..."

"STARSHINE, GET YOUR REAR END OVER HERE THIS MINUTE!! YOU KIDS LEAVE THIS BUILDING IN AN ORDERLY MANNER!" I screamed, using a sentence that came into my brain from somewhere long ago and far away.

Somehow we got out of the pretend fire safely and lined up outdoors, facing the not-burning building. The Public Address system blared,

"Please remain standing silently in your lines, awaiting further directions, until you hear the signal telling you that you may reenter the building."

"Who's the guy on the loud-speaker? Wouldn't he burn to death if this were a real fire? How do they decide who stays inside to make the announcements?" asked a young wag. I looked at him with admiration, because I'd asked the same kinds of questions myself, not too many years ago, but it was caged admiration because now I was the adult. I smiled tolerantly and shushed him.

So there we all were. My class lined up between Madame Hemphill, the French teacher, and Señora Beal, the Spanish teacher. Señora Beal was perfect. She had perfect control over her classes. She seemed to have perfect control over everything. In fact, the principal made me observe Señora Beal's classes in my first week at the school to learn how to be a good teacher.

Señora Beal had her back turned to her class as she wrote "*El burro es un animal importante*" on the blackboard. Susie Wilson, the little red-haired girl known in the faculty lounge as "Pecker," because she jabbed her index finger smartly and constantly into your deltoid muscle when she talked to you, even though she was only eleven years old, started whispering to her neighbor. Señora Beal didn't miss a beat – she kept on writing and said in a voice like Snow White, "No, no, no, *estudiantes* – we don't behave that way *en la clase de español*," and Pecker stopped talking and actually blushed.

Easy. I can do that. So, the first time I turned my back on the class to write on the board and I heard kids talking, I trilled, "No, no, no..." without turning around, but there was so much noise, that no one could hear me. I had to turn around and yell like a regular teacher. So much for a role model.

Not to put too fine a point on things, we were all doing pretty well at the fire drill until a kid I'll call "Stinky" stepped in what I'll call "dog shit." Stinky started yelling, "ARG-H-H! OH, NO-O-O! I STEPPED IN DOG SHIT! HELP!" His classmates, of course, were then all obliged, to a kid, to yell in sympathy.

"Miss Goodman, what should I do?" wailed Stinky. The heck with him," I thought, "What am I going to do — send him back into the allegedly burning building to wash his shoes, or keep him outside to continue yelling and trash the fragile order of things?"

Mr. Doofus strode toward me. "What's all this noise? Miss Goodman, keep your class in order..." he began, but he stepped directly in a doggy dingleberry that Stinky had missed, looked down at his shoe, turned on his slimy heel and walked quickly away without another word. My class looked at me for guidance, but I'm afraid I was no help to them.

"I can't do this with a straight face – I just can't," I thought. The signal to reenter the building sounded at that moment. The signal turned out to be a nine-billion-decibel siren that lifted me three feet straight off the ground.

"WHAT THE HELL WAS THAT?" I screamed to my group of twelve-year-olds.

"Oooo-h-h! Miss Goodman said 'hell!'"

"Yeah, I heard her, too-o-o!"

"I'm telling my parents!"

"Me, too-o-o!" I heard them say as they filed back into study hall, and I knew they meant what they said.

Later that afternoon, I looked in the *Principles, Policies and Practices* teachers' handbook to find out what to do next time, but I couldn't find the chapter about "Dog-Shit, What to Do in Case of..." so I put the unread handbook back in the bottom drawer of my desk to compost for the next twenty-seven years until I retired.

Of course Stinky's mother called the principal to complain that I had used the word "hell" in a school setting, but we shut her up by telling her what her son really said. I had dodged the first of many bullets.

I should have known at the very moment that the shit hit the foot, that I was at the high point of my teaching career and that things could only go downhill from there. I should have thrown my classroom keys and roll book on the grass and kept right on walking away from the building to my car and driven south to Key West and stayed there.

You see a lot of former school teachers in the Keys. People who've been living on the beach for twenty years in the same tattered clothes they wore when they fled after one fire drill or locker inspection or lunchroom duty too many. If they let you get close enough, you can almost tell which subject they taught by the degree of dementia in their eyes.

The Scrapple Experience

By Mike Todd

A little while back, I described my wife's first experiences with scrapple, the meat (and I use the term loosely) product that makes SPAM seem like filet mignon. As if any reason were necessary, I offered that one might do well to steer clear of scrapple solely because I'd never seen my dad eat the stuff.

Nothing fazes the man, culinarily speaking. The nasty yellow stuff inside crabs? Tasty. Caesar salads at fancy restaurants where they sneak in anchovies without even asking you first? His favorite. He can make an entire meal out of the gristle that Mom leaves on her discarded chicken wings. The bones are so clean afterwards that natural history museums buy them to make exhibits. But I honestly believed that the hunt to find something that Dad wouldn't eat had reached its exciting conclusion with scrapple.

Well, Dad took that as a challenge, of course. He got up early one morning and headed down to the local diner, by himself, for his date with pig scrap destiny. The date went well. They've been seeing each other ever since. Dad is now an avid scrappler; he even makes special trips on Saturday mornings to get his eggs and scrapple breakfast. Mom rarely joins him. Laugh and the world laughs with you; eat pig nostrils and you dine alone.

During my most recent visit home, Dad couldn't wait to take me out to breakfast. I reluctantly agreed, knowing that I'd probably regret it. Mom came along this time, if for nothing else than the spectacle.

"I don't see why you two keep talking about scrapple," she said. "You're just trying to gross me out." She was right, of course.

Before we ordered, Dad explained, "Scrapple's like cornbread, but it's meat. It's just a slice of meaty cornbread, and it's kind of crispy." He said this as if he had just given me a reason to try it.

When the server came to take our order, I just couldn't bring myself to do it. I got French toast.

"You can try some of mine," Dad offered graciously.

When our meals came out, I finally came face-to-loaf with the legendary comestible for the first time. It was actually pretty unassuming, with the ingredients prudently chopped so tiny that you couldn't make out which pieces came from hooves. The slab on Dad's plate looked like meat particleboard. Scrapple is the IKEA furniture of breakfast foods. They should serve it with an Allen wrench.

Dad immediately cut off a piece the size of a brick and put it on my plate. I looked down at it and shook my head.

"I don't know if I can do this," I said. "I'm having trouble shutting off my brain."

"Oh, it's just a little piece," Dad said. I realized then that Dad had become the bad kid in the ABC After School Special, pressuring me into trying something I shouldn't be doing. "Go ahead. Try it. You'll like it. First taste's on me."

I submitted, cutting off a small piece and, fork shaking, biting into it. It wasn't bad, really, but I couldn't shake the notion that I'd just put something unspeakably wrong into my mouth, like a kid who'd been talked into eating a slug.

My sister-in-law Jill recently became a vegetarian. I'm pretty sure that I could never be one myself, but I am a vegetarian sympathizer, which means that I respect them, and I try to sit next to them at weddings in case they get served prime rib or something. I can just picture the look of horror on her face if Dad were to order scrapple in front of her.

"What is he eating?" she would whisper to me.

"Um, that's eggplant, Jill," I would tell her. "Every last blessed part of the eggplant."

You can scrape your scrapple onto Mike Todd's plate at mikectodd@gmail.com.

Television is a Talking Dog

By Hugh Gilmore

"Dave. Stop. Stop, Dave. Will you stop, Dave? I'm afraid. I'm afraid, Dave. Dave, my mind is going. I can feel it..." (2001: A Space Odyssey)

Hail Zucker

One of the most intelligent and perceptive writers in our town is Jonathan Storm of The Philadelphia Inquirer. Unfortunately, he labors as their "Television Critic." That means, first of all, that he must take the medium seriously. And it also means he rewrites press releases sent him by the industry, interviews "talent," and watches a lot of TV.

A LOT of TV. Sometimes when he's not reporting—a.k.a. promoting the interests of the greedy cretins who sell Stupid Pills— he actually criticizes a show. In fact, he and his fellow members of the TCA—the Television Critics Association—give out awards every year.

Such times are when I feel most sorry for Mr. Storm, because it seems he has been called in to judge Best of Show from among the pumpkins exhibited at the Chernobyl County Fair. Not that such a job couldn't be challenging: this pumpkin is too lopsided; this one rotten; those three over there—off-color. Ah, here's one that's perfectly round and orange and it thumps well. Let's pin a prize ribbon to its fine ribs, loft it up onto the pedestal, and superglue a laurel wreath to its noble (albeit low) brow.

The 2006 nominees for "Outstanding Achievement in Drama" included Grey's Anatomy, Lost, 24 and House. Grey's Anatomy won. Hugh Laurie, playing the eponymous Greg House, won best dramatic actor. Among the voters were the aforementioned Jonathan Storm and his colleague, Gale Shister (the other Inky TV columnist), two very bright members of the Television Critics Association.

"O, what a noble mind is here o'erthrown!" as Ophelia liked to say when Hamlet put the lampshade on his head and started cutting up.

Well, Television is a fact of modern life, you say, like bare bellybuttons, overly constricted throat-singing, and screaming ads for F.C. Kerbeck. Get used to having your occipital bone lifted so the newly anointed NBC chief, Jeff Zucker, can spray Day-Glo graffiti against the back wall of your brain.

What's bothering me?

Okay, I'll tell you what's bothering me. I've OD'd on the TV show House. Why? Because originally I wanted to be a good sport, and then, when I couldn't manage to be a good sport any longer, because I wanted ammunition for this column.

My son, now 20, is quite the comedy maven. He loved Rowan Atkinson's Black Adder BBC series and got his mom and me to watch it. The two of them loved it and now, like English schoolboys, know large sections by heart. The cast included Hugh Laurie, always playing a bubbly dimwit.

That became "Let's see what kind of role Hugh Laurie has in House." And, "Oh my, our neighbor, David Morse, is in this episode." And, let's rent the DVD, which turned out to be many DVDs, many episodes.

The net effect of this experience is that—this is not a boast—I've seen in the year 2007, concurrent with my vainglorious quest to read 100 books, every episode of House telecasted since the dawn of time, i.e., back when Stanley Kubrick made the bones fly in slow motion to Also Sprach Zarathustra and thus offered pop culture its most overused cliché.

House presents the ongoing story of Dr. Greg House, "Chief Diagnostician" of the soap-opera-ish Princeton/Plainfield Hospital. House is boss of this year's version of the Med-Squad Mod-Squad All-Star-Bod-Squad Differential-Diagnosis and Home-Invasion Team. Phew, that was a mouthful! The underlings add up to three:

One hottie sweet-young-thing doctor who specializes in infectious diseases while wearing 4-inch heels and always standing arms akimbo like Wonder Woman. She's the conscience.

One Aussie surfer doctor guy—he specializes in liver surgery. Oh, and spinal cord surgery. Oh and hoof and mouth disease.

And there's another doctor guy, African-American, who worked his way up from the ghet-tow. He's smart as a whip and knowledgeable, but House likes to count on him for sneaking into the stupid patients' houses to search for environmental toxins or contaminants that the stupid patients won't or don't know have caused their disease.

Oh, that House, he's such a stitch, forget the Constitution, he knows what's good for you!

Oh, yes, forgot: House won't take anything but the most puzzling, mysterious, anomalous cases, the sort a doctor of infectious diseases might see once in a lifetime. He's rude. He's weird. He literally talks, when he's sarcastic, like a teenage girl, what Tom Wolfe described in I Am Charlotte Simmons as "Sarc 3." House is also petty, lazy, addicted to Vicodin, and self-centered. His behaviors are tolerated and he keeps his job because He's Always Right. Because He's The Best There Is At What He Is. And he's Damned Good At It Too! —At Being The Best There is! that is.

And they all know whenever he gets an important insight because he grunts and then limps away from them (he has a motive-supplying pained leg). They then have to run down the hall after him while he talks to them like they're idiots—or mere actors.

Why 24 Million People Like Him

The latest Neilsen ratings place House second only to American Idol at 24,000,00 households. I've not managed to talk to most of those people as to why yet, but my sample of people who like the show reveals:

(1)"Oh the things he does and says. They're so outrageous."

(He acts out people's vicarious desire to be rude. You can almost count on him to insult the race, creed, physical deformity, or disease of everyone he meets, in order to "snap them out of it" and cure them. Right out of Punch and Judy.)

(2) "It's intelligent. They discuss the cases at a high level and keep you guessing."

(The script team creates the show right from the diagnostic manual, spouts multi-syllabic gibberish as fast as it can humanly be said, gives you lots of false clues, and withholds the clinching fact till the end.)

(3) "Hugh Laurie is such a good actor. I didn't even know he was English till I heard him on a talk show. He does a great American accent." (A weird one. The directors help by making all his speeches happen in snippy little phrases so he doesn't have to sustain the accent. Further, his American voice is spoken from a face doing English facial

expressions, making for a weird, offbeat effect. Another factor is that Laurie has a wonderful rubbery comic's face, but is directed for this show to keep it still and do lots of staring, knowing staring, so the same clown face, seen in repose, is handsome until he starts talking again.)

(4) "Even though he's rude and mean, if you had a rare disease, you'd want him for your doctor, wouldn't you?" (Sure, lady, and if you forgot your apartment keys, and you were dating Spiderman, he could just walk up the side of the building and go in your 12th floor window for you. That's what comic book Superheroes do, isn't it?)

Why I Don't Like It

I don't like anything obviously written from a formula by a team of writers. The novelty achieved is like that created by playing with Mr. (or Mrs.) Potato Head, or one of those games where you turn the flaps of a book in novel sequences. After the initial "Gee, this guy's a regular platypus," I reach for my yawn-snuffler. Let's face it folks, House is a cartoon.

I'm not a complete crank, by the way. If I could enjoy it, I would enjoy it. I feel the same way about screw-top wine.

Television critics are like lonely travelers trapped by a snowstorm in a low dive. They look around for someone to talk to, or at least watch. And lo and behold … there's a talking dog!

So they listen. Isn't this amazing? This dog talks. So they start taking notes. And the dog keeps talking. He's handing out press releases. Stamping paw marks on his 8 x 10 glossies. The dog has a lousy vocabulary though, and he mispronounces lots of words. And his stories are smutty. And often involve biting. In fact, he's a complete bore, but, gee, I mean, it's a talking dog. That's amazing.

That's what people mean when they refer to a certain show as "Good TELevision." "24" is "Good TELevision." "'House' is Good TELevision."

No one has to say The Grapes of Wrath is "Good BOok."

It's good to take candy bars on life's picnic, but only candy bars?

When do we start our grown-up lives? …When death pries the remote control from our cold dead hands?

To the New College Graduates

By Jim Harris

Your parents have just spent their entire retirement fund on your education, and you now owe it to them to obtain a high-paying job so that you can make them proud and support them in their doddering old age.

But seriously, you really do need to get a job quickly before you forget all of that educational stuff that you presumably learned in college between keg parties and panty raids. Of course, the age-old, traditional way of doing that is by using the venerable "Yellow Pages." This massive opus, many years in the making, has a complete alphabetical listing of every potential employer in the area.

So, for example, if you had a degree in Business, you would look under "Retail," and locate all the "Gap" stores (there are seven in Chestnut Hill alone) to begin your search. If your degree is in English or Liberal Arts, you'd check out "Restaurants" to find your niche as a witty waiter, waitress, or bartender. If you are a Phys Ed graduate, you should probably look under "Health Food Restaurants."

If, however, you are a Psychology major, you can safely assume that you will wind up in one of the area's prestigious "Mental Institutions," and If you took Medieval Studies, you can save a lot of time by just going ahead and registering right now with the "Department of Public Assistance."

When you have contacted a prospective employer, you will be required to go in for an interview. The following are a few of my "can't-miss" tips and techniques for impressing your future employers.

In nature, animals always "puff up" to impress the other animals. Likewise, if you stuff your clothes with tissue paper, wear a big teased wig, and do whatever else you can to appear larger-than-life, you will gain the immediate admiration and respect of your interviewer. Also, when you enter the interview room, you should be talking on three cell phones at once, pretending to be receiving other job offers. In fact, don't just talk - yell, and try to emit sounds from as many orifices as possible simultaneously.

You should smell strongly of musk (available at hunting–supply shops), and carry a tape recorder in your pocket playing bullfighting music. It's also a good idea to have blinking lights on your tie or necklace, and, if you can arrange it, have a spokesperson do all of your communicating with the interviewer for you, while you nonchalantly smoke a cigarette and nod approvingly.

If an interviewer should ask you (or your spokesperson) where you see yourself in five years, gesture wildly and shout something grandiose, like "I would like to rule the world." You will be praised as if you had actually already accomplished this feat, and in five years, no one will even remember that you said it, anyway.

It's also good to have a resume. It can be based loosely on reality, but it doesn't have to be. The main purpose is to showcase your creativity. Make sure that all of your "facts" are hard to verify. For example, "Spent the summer tutoring Himalayan villagers in modern Yak-breeding techniques," and include any awards you may have won, even if you personally created them and gave them to yourself.

A few excerpts from my own extensive resume might be in order here:

• Board certified member of the American Academy of This N' That

• Honorary PhD in Scientific Sciences from the Prague Institute of Learning

• Current Director of the Group for the Study of the Study of Groups.

As a self-made man, I learned early that one must be determined and resourceful to succeed in life. Even though I was not initially accepted into Harvard University — I never even actually applied — I went there anyway, and spent six years lurking in cloakrooms and masquerading as a maintenance man. It was tough, and there were times when I almost felt like giving up, but in the end, I persevered, and when I finally left Harvard in a moving ceremony conducted by several Cambridge police officers, I had learned skills which would sustain me for years to come.

I'm proud to say that my son Nimrod has just finished his third year hiding in a lawnmower shed at UCLA, and next September, our daughter Galactica will enter Bryn Mawr college — through a laundry chute! Truly, the apple doesn't crawl far from the tree.

So in closing, I would say this to you who are about to graduate: a mind is a terrible thing to waste, but you have to keep trying. We're counting on you.

Penny Rebellion

By Janet Gilmore

Mark "Rags" Raginsky wasn't a bad kid. His big sister thought he was a pest, but his parents loved him. He did his chores mostly when he was asked and got good grades in school. But his friends knew what he was capable of in the right circumstances.

So when he came up with The Idea, none of the guys in his room were surprised.

"What do you think?" he asked.

"You're crazy, Raginsky," said Raytek. "They'll throw the book at us and we'll all be in 8th grade forever. Forget it."

"It's a good idea, Rags," said Cheeks, "but I don't know, what's the point?"

"Just for a joke," said Rags. "We'll start saving today, and by April Fool's Day, we should have enough to pay for our lunches with pennies. What do you think? Pretty good, huh?"

"April Fool's day is on a Friday," said Cheeks, who could calculate things like that in his mind. We're going to get caught, but they might not get a chance to tell our parents until Monday, so at least we'll have the weekend... Let me think about it."

"They can't expel you from school, can they?" asked Raytek. I mean, it's only a joke, right?"

"Yeah," said Cheeks. "They'll probably give us a detention or something and we can serve it together, so that might be okay."

"I'm in," said Goff. "It'll be great! Drive Doofus crazy! Let's do it!" No wonder Raginsky loved Goff the most of all his friends.

Mr. Dunstan Doofus, Master of Education, head of bone, heart of stone, was the vice principal at Fairplay Middle School. He was a hairy, twitchy man who prided himself on running a tight ship on the job. At the very moment the Penny Rebellion was being planned, he was in his bathroom, brushing his teeth carefully, preparing to sleep the sleep of a man who had kept things under control all week and could finally relax. He was trying not to think about the kids smoking in the woods behind the building. He knew they were doing it, but by the time he got to the back, the kids had already been warned by the kid-grapevine and moved somewhere else around the building, or finished their smokes.

It drove him crazy. But, as he put the cap back on the toothpaste, a wisp of an idea occurred to him. As he put his arm into the first pajama sleeve, he thought his idea was very good. At the second sleeve, he thought it might be brilliant. As he buttoned the last button under his chin, he knew it was the idea of the century, and would certainly get him an interview, and possibly the cover story in *Where Are You Going? The Magazine of Hall Pass Innovation.* He slept deeply and dreamt about the scales of justice, tipped in his favor.

Raginsky started saving pennies. He looked at the bottom of his book bag. Found three pennies under a squashed cheese sandwich that seemed to have green alfalfa sprouts on it, but didn't. He also found his retainer and the Spanish homework he didn't hand in last month. He put the pennies in a sock he found on the floor and was under way.

Monday, the boys were standing around outside at recess, shivering in the cold winter air. Kids weren't allowed to wear coats or hats in the building, for never-explained reasons known only to Mr. Doofus, and very punishable. Kids were allowed to get their hats and coats to go outside during recess, but doing that took ten precious minutes of free time, so most kids skipped the outerwear and ran outside immediately. On this particular day, Raginsky and his friends huddled close, talking.

"How's the penny collection?" asked Raytek.

"Good. I found 3 in my book bag, a few in my sister's room, more on my parents' night tables, and I asked them to change a few nickels for me. They asked why, so I told them we're doing a project on the U.S. Mint. I have 38¢ already!"

"You're crazy," said Raytek. "You're gonna get in so much trouble."

"Want to pencil fight?" asked Goff.

"Sure, got some pencils?"

"Not me," said Cheeks, throwing peanuts up in the air and catching them expertly in his mouth.

A seagull flew overhead. A lone, lucky seagull, who knew how school buildings were at recess. Cheeks saw the seagull and a glint of something else.

"What's that?" he said, pointing up.

Eight young eyes looked up and saw, at the same moment, the glint of March sunlight reflecting off the edge of Mr. Doofus' binoculars.

The boys didn't quite believe what they saw. They looked at each other without saying a word. They looked up again. They saw what they saw. Doofus, in an expensive overcoat and a red wool cap with snowflakes on it that his mother had knit for him, was on the roof of their school.

"What is he doing?"

"Why is he up on the roof?"

They heard other kids talking.

"Who is that?"

"Doofus."

"What's he doing up there?"

"Trying to fly, I hope."

"What's he got on his shoulder?"

"What are you talking about?"

"You mean the binoculars?"

"No, the other thing. Look!"

And sure enough, Mr. Doofus had turned 90° away from Raginsky and his friends and was peering intently into the woods behind the school. He put down the binoculars and picked up the *bull horn*, which he had carried up to the roof on a shoulder strap, and bellowed into it, "You kids down there! I see you smoking and I know who you are! I want you all to report to my office immediately!" The more religious smokers feared that God the Father himself was scolding them directly from heaven, and were surprised to hear that He had an office in their school. Young agnostics knew what was going on immediately. Not God, but Doofus.

Raginsky and his friends couldn't believe their eyes and ears. They began to laugh the laugh of the totally powerless – the kind of helpless laugh whose natural conclusion is knees buckling, kids falling down and staying down for a long time until the waves of hilarity ebbed completely, but just as their knees weakened, the bell rang and recess was over. They staggered back into the building, still roaring, trying to compose themselves for the next class. Luckily, they were in separate classes that period. On the way in, Cheeks, who had just beheld and grasped the true meaning of junior high school and could barely speak for laughing, gasped, "Rags, I'm in!"

"In what?"

"The pennies…" said Cheeks on his way into American Civilization class.

Rags, Cheeks and Goff were ready by April Fool's Day. Raytek never agreed — said his parents would kill him if he got in trouble.

Rags was first in the lunch line that day. He went through, got his tray filled with mammal noodle casserole, stewed tomatoes, French fries, milk and a pink foamy dessert item that clung upside down to the monkey dish no matter how long he held it that way. When he got to the cash register, he pulled the sock from his book bag and poured 250 pennies onto the counter.

"What's this?" the lunch lady demanded.

"My lunch money."

"You can't pay in pennies."

"Why not?"

The lunch lady turned abruptly on her sensible rubber heel and went to get her supervisor.

"What's this?" asked the supervisor.

"My lunch money," said Rags.

"You can't pay in pennies."

"Why not?"

And a small, sensible question from a hungry peasant might have toppled a mighty cafeteria. But behind the counter and back in the school kitchen, hairnets were conferring with one another. Large bags of budget meat extender sat unused on counters. The large machine with the hook in it, continued turning, unattended, mixing the following day's tuna fish and mayonnaise into a lunch. The ladies didn't know what to do.

The younger teachers were in the teacher cafeteria line, listening, wishing they had thought of the joke themselves, but they were too old, even at age twenty-one. They had jobs now, would never be totally carefree again. The older teachers were incensed, tut-tutting to each other about the end of civilization. Everyone heard Raginsky ask again, "Why not?"

A cafeteria worker phoned the Main Office.

"The first kid in the lunch line is trying to pay for his lunch in pennies!" the white-knuckled woman yelled into the phone. "Send Dunstan down here right away!"

"Pennies?" repeated the secretary, a sensible, intelligent woman, as they often are. "What's the problem? It's probably an April Fool's joke!"

"WHAT'S THE PROBLEM? The problem is…they can't…we don't…nobody ever…shouldn't…if we let one kid pay…JUST SEND DOOFUS!" screamed the lunch lady.

Dunstan Doofus came running at full speed into the cafeteria, dewlaps flapping, drooling a little in anticipation, looking for all the world, like a Saint Bernard dog trying to save a lunch line about to be buried under an avalanche of pennies, with a barrel of detentions tied around his neck.

Without actually sizing up the problem, he grabbed the microphone. There was no question of natural consequence. No thought that the 150 hungry kids behind Raginsky might get impatient, start pushing forward a bit, the cafeteria lady could tell Raginsky to step aside, she didn't have time to count his change now, she'd just serve the other kids and get back to him after everyone else had their lunch. No thought that the whole thing might be a joke, that Raginsky might have $2.50 on him in normal money, just in case.

Doofus used his loudest outdoor voice in the microphone. He thought at the time that a microphone in a large cafeteria put him in his optimal setting, sort of his dream setting, his amphitheater, where he could out-shout anyone.

He would have to remember that for later. He took his opportunity to holler, "ALL OF YOU KIDS, STOP WHAT YOU'RE DOING! LET ME TELL YOU THAT ANYONE, **ANYONE** CAUGHT PAYING FOR LUNCH WITH PENNIES WILL BE SUSPENDED FROM SCHOOL AND SENT HOME FOR TWO DAYS! DO YOU UNDERSTAND? THIS IS ABSOLUTELY UNACCEPTABLE BEHAVIOR!"

Tiny voices here and there said, "April Fool's!" but they were either ignored or not heard. One of the younger teachers was heard to say, "I'd love to get sent home for two days – anyone have any pennies?"

Doofus went on, "I WILL NOW ASK THE CAFETERIA LADIES TO POINT OUT TO ME THE STUDENTS WHO

TRIED TO PAY WITH PENNIES AND THOSE STUDENTS WILL BE DEALT WITH SEVERELY! THE REST OF YOU ARE TO GO THROUGH THE LINE IN AN ORDERLY WAY AND GET YOUR LUNCH! APRIL FOOL'S DAY IS NOT A TIME FOR JOKES!"

The only thing Raginsky could do was refuse to name anyone else in on the plot, which he did. Some younger kids ratted out Cheeks and Goff. The rest of the kids ate their lunch. The smokers looked at each other and grinned, realizing that Doofus would be busy processing penny-payers for the rest of the period, so they sauntered outside for a leisurely cigarette. Afternoon teachers had a little bit of trouble getting classes started, but basically the revolution was quashed.

Goff and Raginsky's parents were friends, and they all worked outside the house. They decided that it would be safer if the boys stayed together at Goff's house for their two days of suspension. Which suited the boys just fine.

Dunstan Doofus went home happy from school that weekend. He had put a big, hairy thumb on the neck of a dangerous rebellion and killed it. He knew, though, that junior high was a mercurial place. You could settle one problem and, like quicksilver, it would break into thousands of pieces and spread all over and grow into new problems. But he was secure that he got it all this time and there would be no more tomfoolery on his watch. April Fool.

You've Lost a Friend in Pennsylvania

By Mike Todd

Getting my mom to join Facebook seemed like such a good idea at the time. In retrospect, it was an innovation on par with New Coke, the Hindenburg and The Matrix sequels.

"Oh, that's for you kids. You don't want me lurking around on Facebook, seeing what you all are up to," she said a few weeks ago. Up to that point, Mom's favorite social networking site had been her living room.

But my wife Kara and I insisted, thinking that Mom would enjoy using Facebook, catching up with some old friends and keeping up with current ones. So during a weekend visit to our house, while my dad and I huddled around the kitchen sink, trying to figure out the right combination of expletives and wrenches to get the new faucet installed, Kara and Mom huddled around the laptop, working on installing Mom into the world of online social networking.

Initially, the installation looked very promising. "Ooh, hey, I haven't talked to her since high school!" Mom said, high-fiving Kara as they trolled through Facebook's oceans of people, chumming friend requests overboard along the way. By the end of the weekend, Mom had connected with a couple dozen friends and family members. Your Facebook account isn't fully mature until it gathers more friends than the number of people you've actually met in your life, but it was a good start.

The troubles began later in the week, when Mom changed her relationship status to "Married" to reflect her forty-one years of marriage to my dad.

Immediately, some family friends from my generation posted comments like: "Congratulations on finally getting him to tie the knot!" and "Hubba hubba -- who's the new beau?"

"They're making fun of me," Mom said over the phone. "What did I do wrong?"

"Nothing, Mom. They were just joking around," I said.

"Well, okay, but I don't really understand the point of all this. Your cousin just told the whole world what he ate for breakfast," she said.

"You don't have to read everybody's status updates," I replied.

"I had Special K with fresh blueberries this morning. Do you think I should tell everyone?" she asked.

Clearly, her generation lacks the healthy narcissism of mine. Mom's enthusiasm for Facebook gradually waned over the next few days as waves of shallow communications washed across her screen. Then a family friend uploaded a picture of Mom in which she'd been caught mid-sentence, clearly not ready for the flash to go off. It was the upload that broke the camel's back.

"I've been trying for three hours to delete this photo of me," she said, sounding exhausted. "How do I get rid of it?"

Unfortunately, pictures from your past, uploaded by your friends, are an indignity one must suffer as a Facebook user. A friend of mine from college recently uploaded pictures of me from the regrettable period several months after I'd decided to grow my hair out. Growing your hair long isn't something you just do. It takes lots of dedication and baseball caps.

The first comment read like this: "Hey, Mike looks like a mushroom. Look out, Mike! Super Mario's going to jump on you!"

I tried to explain to Mom that she couldn't delete pictures that she hadn't uploaded. The best she could do was to remove the tag that contained her name.

"Well, I don't think Facebook was meant for my generation. I'm going to leave," she said.

"Leave? I don't think you can leave," I said. "It's like the mafia."

Somehow, though, Mom left. I picture her dropping from the ceiling at Facebook headquarters, suspended from the small of her back by a cable like Tom Cruise in Mission: Impossible.

If you'd like to issue a friend request to my mom these days, the best place to start would probably be her living room.

You can de-friend Mike Todd at mikectodd@gmail.com.

Writing the Soft-Boiled Crime Novel

By Hugh Gilmore

True Story, I swear:

I was about five or six years old, ya know? And this neighborhood kid my own age was buggin' me. I don't know what he was doin', pinching me maybe. My uncle (let's say 'Louie') was sittin' on the lawn in his lawn chair. Right behind us.

I says, "Unc, this kid 'Tommy' is pinchin' me."

Uncle Louie looks at me. He looks at Tommy. He gets a fresh idea look on his face. He stands up.

He lines me up in front of Tommy, face-to-face.

Uncle Louie says to me, "Punch him."

I'm like, "Whoa." I'm expecting some adult intervention here, some relief from the childhood jungle.

So I tell him, "Huh?"

Unc says, "Punch him. Punch him in the mouth."

I look at Tommy. Tommy looks at me. He's puzzled too.

Unc says, "You said he was pinchin' you. You want him to stop? Punch him in the mouth."

I had no desire to punch Tommy in the mouth. He was just an annoying kid being an annoying kid. I wanted my uncle to tell Tommy not to pinch me any more. Tommy just stood there like an obedient child who'd been told, "Go stand on the trolley tracks, the No. 36 is coming."

Everyone froze, listening in that silence that usually precedes sparks, until it became obvious no one was hittin' anyone today. We all dissolved away from the scene.

Three kinds of shame followed. Uncle Louie had to live related (by marriage) to a kid with no spunk. Tommy slunk away knowing he'd been exposed as a pincher. And I discovered, for the first time, that I lacked the guts to pull the trigger.

As it were.

The same problem plagues me now as a first-time crime/suspense/mystery novel writer.

I've had a very hard time punching anyone in the mouth. I mean, having my characters do so. This is not a good trait to possess when you're writing in this vein. Readers have come to expect that you create a bunch of expendable people, stuff them in a big Cuisinart and start tapping the "Pulse" button.

This week, writing since January 1, I finished the first major draft of my book — about 120,000 words. I created characters who, no matter how badly they behaved, I started feeling sorry for because I understood their lives and their points of view. Oh, don't get me wrong, I managed to kill a few of them, but I didn't enjoy it. Four people bit the dust, but, sadly, only one of them was innocent. The other three killings were all retributive. Satisfying, but will it sell?

The main problem is that I could not get my main character out of trouble by having him feed knuckle sandwiches to the baddies and the wannabes. His consciousness came too deeply out of my own. Whenever he was threatened in the book, he talked his way out of trouble, or bluffed, or escaped. Not once did he take off a holster or set aside his knives and num-chuks and get in a fistfight. If I'd made him do that, I'd cringe in fear of anyone who knows me saying, "Taking to writing Walter Mitty stories now, have you, Hugh?"

Gee, though, maybe I could.

I'll practice by rewriting the scene with Tommy and Uncle Louie out on the lawn, back when I was five or six.

How's this:

Take Two

I was out on the lawn on a summer evening. A local wiseguy, we'll call Tommy Pinch-Pinch pulls up. He's big. I mean big. The guy's got arms up the wazoo, you know, like slabs of beef, and thumbs like a freakin' lobstah.

"Hey, what choo doin' 'round here?" I says.

"Mind yer own falootin' bizness," he says.

"This *is* my bizness," I says. I take off my black silk jacket. I take off my black silk tie. I'm down to my black silk muscle shirt. I tuck in my gold chains.

We stand toe-to-toe. Tommy makes the first move. He reaches

out and pinches my tricep. Hurts like a dingbat, but I don't let on. I'm ready to haul off.

Carmella comes runnin' up. "Don't do it Youee, take it to Uncle Louie, the Don."

Why not? He's right here. In fact, Tommy and I are blockin' his view of the Lawn Darts game between the Chinolli brothers and their cousins.

I say, "Unc, Don, whatever, Tommy here isn't even supposed to be here and here he is ... here ... ya know what I mean? And he's pinchin' my arm."

Don Unc looks at me, looks at Tommy, shakes his head sadly, says, "Is this true?"

Tommy says, "I been pinchin' his arm thirty years, *now* it's a problem?"

That does it. Childhood memories are brought back. I snap.

I don't even wait. I throw a vicious left hook to Uncle Louie's bicep. He scrunches up. I grab his collar and start pinchin' his cheeks, precision pinchin', trying to leave welts so it looks like a mudpie face.

"Okay, Unc," I say, "that's for not backin' me when I was a kid." He falls out of his lawn chair.

Tommy, he's running for the car. Funniest thing you ever seen. He gets in and lays a patch gettin' out of there. His lobster claws're white from gripping the steering wheel so hard.

I freagin' laughed so hard I hardly had the breath to tell Carmella, "Yo, babe, bring me a beer ... and another piece of that freagin' quiche."

I'm hungry like you wouldn't believe.

Okay. I think the rewrites for my crime book are going to be easy now ... if I can just keep up that kind of nerve.

Jobs for Dead People

By Jim Harris

According to the Swedish newspaper *Expressen*, General Motors' Saab division has recently been using human cadavers in scientific crash tests. "For certain things, it's important to use cadavers," said Caes Tingvall of the Swedish Road Administration.

Wow! Attitudes have certainly changed since the days when Leonardo da Vinci had to obtain bodies for his anatomical studies under cover of night to avoid being labeled a witch. Academia and industry now make copious use of cadavers in all sorts of innovative ways.

The show "The Amazing Body" has been touring the country, raking in money and employing dozens of denizens of Deadsville, and the success of TV shows like CSI and the proliferation of "cadaver farms" for forensic research testify to the rabid fascination with all things dead in society today.

I think it's marvelous that people are no longer letting death stop them from being active members of the community. According to "Modern Corpse" magazine, "Dead is now the new fifty." Airports and malls already have moving sidewalks to accommodate the dead, and new laws are being written to protect the rights of those who, through no fault of their own, find themselves decomposing. Full–time jobs for the dead are still pretty scarce, however, and what is available is usually either menial or deadly boring.

Mort Kaputski, president of the Philadelphia Deceased Citizen's Alliance (PDCA) says, "I want to be able to look at every sector of the job market and be able to say, 'I see dead people.' Just because a person is not breathing does not mean that he or she should not be working." A recently released PDCA report outlined a number of positions that it claimed could be filled by expired individuals.

Jobs in the field of public safety included front man in a toboggan, bulletproof shield, and battering ram. In the entertainment industry, it was suggested that deceased actors could play dead people in movies. According to Kaputski, "Having live actors portray cadavers is not only silly, but insulting when there are so many unemployed dead actors just waiting for jobs."

The report went on to say, "The dead can be employed to fill empty audience seats at TV award shows, and they make excellent puppets as well. And just imagine if that statue of Ben Franklin at the Constitution Center actually *were* Ben Franklin. What an unforgettable impression that would make upon a curious child. Previously-alive individuals also make excellent psychiatrists and psychotherapists. They're great listeners, they never hit on their clients, and the only thing they can't do that a live psychiatrist can do is charge you lots of money." Other potentially viable vocations listed included piñata, boat anchor, paperweight, doorstop, elevator counterbalance, and scarecrow.

So forget all that crap you were taught in school about your body being a temple, folks. Your body is merely an incredibly utilitarian contraption of endless possibility, a gift to future generations to use as they see fit, for business, pleasure and wondrous purposes beyond our wildest imagination.

On a practical note, if you haven't started already, you should begin planning now for your dead years. In addition to your retirement IRA, you should have an RIP account for all of your post-life expenses, so as not to pose a burden to your loved ones.

And don't keep postponing it, thinking that your demise is a long way off. Señor Death can sneak up on you like a panhandler at a traffic light and terminate your lease on life before you know what hit you. In fact, you could already be dead and not even know it. According to the President's Council on Deadness, the signs that you may be dead can include loss of appetite, trouble completing even simple tasks, and watching excessive amounts of TV, especially talk shows.

If you think you might be dead, have yourself laminated as soon as possible, and above all, don't consider it a death sentence. Well, okay you can consider it a death sentence, but think of it as one ending with a semicolon rather than a period. So keep your chin up, your chest out, and remember, every day's a holiday when you're dead.

Just Wishin' and Hopin' and Thinkin' and Dreamin', Plannin' and Bowlin'

By Janet Gilmore

Once upon a time, a beautiful princess kept steady company in college and four years thereafter, with a troll I nicknamed Sneezy because of his resemblance to Snow White's dwarf of the same name. I was not head over heels in love with him, but I assumed you married your college boyfriend, even if he refused to go to Woodstock because he didn't think he'd find a parking space.

"Sneezy, do you ever think about getting married?" I asked in year #1 of our relationship.

"Don't EVER give me an ultimatum!" he said. I took that as a 'no'.

We graduated. I was desperate to get married, since I didn't have a job lined up. I was ready. I always wanted a family, especially if it meant bypassing a job.

Sneezy lived in Yonkers with his parents. After graduation, we each got a teaching job, mine locally, Sneezy's in the Bronx. We fell into a commuting relationship, me traveling to Yonkers every weekend. Sneezy mostly worked on his beloved 1967 Pontiac Firebird on Saturday afternoons. If I held out my ringless left hand, he put a wrench in it and asked me to hold it. We went bowling or to a movie at night.

We went to lots of friends' weddings. Every time I mentioned marriage, though, Sneezy either yelled at me or stuck his head back under the hood of his car.

Year #3, my Dad, trying to do the right fatherly thing, sent Sneezy a letter saying that if money were the impediment to our getting married, he would be glad to help. My father offering to pay my boyfriend to marry me was a new humiliation. And money wasn't the problem.

Over five years of whining, pleading, crying and thoroughly embarrassing myself, I had accepted many presents, none of which I

55

wanted. Nice stationery, sweaters, earrings and a coffee-maker do not equal a diamond engagement ring and they never will.

In year #5, a friend of Sneezy's told me in confidence — (*Don't tell him I told you*) — that Sneezy was having my hand measured. "Having your hand measured" seemed like an odd way to say, "Getting you a ring," but once the phrase was in my mind, I started playing with it until it meant what I hoped.

Finally! I told my sister I thought I was getting engaged for Valentine's Day. Of course, she told my parents, who told everybody.

The Saturday before Valentine's Day, Sneezy took me to a bowling alley in the Bronx.

"The bowling alley?" I thought. "I guess they also sell jewelry. Sneezy sure knows how to find a bargain..."

Everyone seemed to know that something was up.

"Hi, Sneezy!"

"Hi, Vinny – this is Janet. You know (wink)..."

Vinny led us to a small back room.

"Here she is," Vinny said. "Tommy, this is Janet."

"Hi, Sneezy. Nice to meet you, Jan," he growled to me. "Let's see your hand."

"My hand..." I held out my hand. I was thrilled to find out what it felt like to become engaged to be married.

"You left-handed?" Tommy asked.

"Yes, I am."

He got a device and measured the distance between my fingers.

"Okay," he said. "You want your name on it?"

"Huh?"

"On your ball – you want your name on it?"

"What ball?" I asked.

"Your bowling ball!" he said, impatiently. "Oh it's a surprise? Sorry, there, Sneezy. I thought you knew — Sneezy is getting you — not just any bowling ball, but a Columbia *Black Knight* — top of the line! You're gonna love it! We're gonna custom-drill the holes right now and put your name on it!"

I suddenly became aware of bowling balls thundering down the lanes in the next room, pinsetter machines re-setting, and the smell of rented bowling shoes. Everyone was so happy for me. Except me.

When I carried my new, shiny, not-a-diamond-ring ball, with

"JANET" stamped on it in gold letters, out to the car that Sneezy loved, I wanted to put it through his @#%^&* windshield.

We put my new ball in the back seat and went to a Chinese restaurant for lunch. When we pulled up in the driveway of Sneezy's parents' house afterward, I barfed Egg Foo Yung all over his car, which made me feel a lot better. I didn't help him clean it up. I took an angry nap instead.

The bowling ball was the last straw. I hated bowling. I hated Sneezy. I might have managed a game or two on Couple's Night, though, as Mister-and-Missus-Married-Bowlers.

Sunday night, I had to carry the ball back to Philadelphia on the train, and tell my father, mother, Aunt Sylvia, Aunt Betty, Aunt Marilyn, Aunt Doris, Aunt Bea, Aunt Burt and my sister that I would not be moving to Yonkers after all — it wasn't a ring, it was a bowling ball. Worse, I had to go back to work on Monday. The ball found a dusty home in a closet and Sneezy was sent on his way.

Many years later, a beau offered me a gold necklace. I looked at it, looked at him. I really liked him and didn't want to offend. "It's beautiful," I said, "but I don't wear gold jewelry. I hardly wear jewelry at all; I don't like things jingling on me. But thank you very much anyway."

"You're kidding," he answered. "You're the only woman I ever met who said that. Okay, I'll return it."

He proposed marriage the next night. I accepted.

"Would you like an engagement ring?" he asked.

"I would love one," I answered.

My husband and I sold the hated bowling ball at a garage sale for $3 to a left-handed man whose name, I guess, was Janet.

Janet Gilmore wants to hear from anyone who has memories of the Pit and/ or the Palace bowling alleys in Mount Airy. And love to Lovett Library Writers' Group for all help.

The Corniest Controversy of All

By Mike Todd

If the reader(s) of this column have come to expect anything, it's probably regular disappointment. But after that, it's probably white-hot controversy, stirred up by my special brand of hard-hitting journalism that's not afraid to shake up the establishment with daring exposes on the cuteness of my puppy.

Last week, though, I'm afraid that even by this column's semblance of standards, I took things a little too far, and one line in particular drew the attention of that vigilant media watchdog, the Corn Refiners Association. Some people will tell you that, as a pretend journalist, you're not really doing your job unless you're occasionally getting under the husk of Big Corn, but I can't help but feel that there might be a kernel of misunderstanding on the cob of this dispute.

Here's the statement from last week's column that perked up the ears of Corn: "The allure of Swedish Fish is either due to the lasting appeal of an age-old recipe, or the fact that high fructose corn syrup can turn your average child into a less-discerning gourmand than your average goat."

As you might have guessed, the main purpose of that sentence was to show off that I could use the word "gourmand" in context, once I'd looked it up on dictionary.com to make sure it didn't mean some kind of fancy gourd.

But a short time after the column ran, I got an email from my editor on a non-deadline day, which didn't seem right. Emails from my editor usually go like this: "Mike, I needed your column three hours ago. Please send me whatever you have."

To which I'll respond, "It will be there momentarily. I'm very close to starting it."

But this time, he was forwarding me a letter from Audrae Erickson, the president of the Corn Refiners Association, who was worried that my column "may mislead consumers about high fructose corn syrup," which is the last thing in the world I'd ever want to do, besides watch another episode of America's Next Top Model, no matter how much my wife insists that I'll like this one.

As a lifelong aficionado of high fructose corn syrup, mostly in Skittle form, it was never my intention to mislead anyone into thinking that the consumption of this delicious (and nutritionally equivalent to sugar!) sweetener could be harmful, or should be moderated, in any way.

Due to my carelessness, casual readers may have arrived at the conclusion that high fructose corn syrup could, in some instances, turn children into goats. To my knowledge, this usually does not occur, though I have seen it turn them into raving lunatics who can't seem to stop spinning in circles while singing the only two words they know to "La Cucaracha."

If I have learned anything from this experience, it is to finally heed the advice of the wise folks who told me to stay away from sensitive topics in this column, topics that people may very well never agree upon, like the death penalty, abortion and Swedish Fish. Some people just won't see the humor in jokes about Swedish Fish, especially people who make a living by not seeing the humor in jokes about Swedish Fish. These people apparently live in Washington, D.C., not Sweden, as you might have expected. They are also probably having dinner with your senator right now.

So I hope you, as a consumer, are now more educated about high fructose corn syrup, and will start demanding it in keg form at every opportunity. For me to believe that high fructose corn syrup is anything other than an enhancer of life's simple joys, I'd have to be dumber than ethanol subsidies.

In the interest of drumming up more controversy for next week, let me just add that soybeans are kind of gross.

You can teach Mike Todd the rest of "La Cucaracha" at mikectodd@gmail.com.

Television In Waiting Rooms

By Hugh Gilmore

This Day Last Year: The Phone Rings

My general fantasy about 5:30 a.m. phone calls is to not answer. It can't be good news. But since my son is away at school and my mother-in-law might need us, I picked up.

My nineteen year-old son, blind in one eye as a result of "retinopathy of the premature," was saying he thought the retina in his "good" eye was detaching. He sensed a shadow, like a window shade drawing, in the corner of his eye. We knew what that meant from seven years ago when two retina surgeries failed to save his left eye. Up we sprang to gather him from Arcadia University nearby and dash to Wills Eye Hospital.

From my wife, Janet's, journal that night:

"I packed a few clothes, some audio tapes and iPod for Andrew to take to the hospital. Looked around his room and saw the wealth of books and videos he's collected so carefully over the years to enhance his knowledge of comedy, and started to well up at the thought that he might never be able to read or watch movies again."

At the hospital, the usual insurance hassles and red tape kept us in the waiting room much longer than my nerves could stand. I said, at different intervals, to three different receptionists, "Look, I'll pay cash for someone to look at my son's eye. Time is the enemy. He needs to be seen." This plea brought sympathetic nods, but no obvious actions. Things move so slowly in emergency situations.

Except when it's their emergency.

As in: "Sir, Don't touch that!"

"Sir, what are you doing, sir?"

"Leave that alone, sir."

They'd all cupped their phones, or dropped their clipboards to stare, while she barked to stop me from turning down the TV.

The whole time we'd been waiting, the reception room television spewed audio pollution at us. Good Morning America. Pretend news shilling for the guests' new moneymaking ventures. Such loud, awful noise. No one was looking at it, so I'd walked over and reached to lower the sound. The staff reacted as though I'd tried to kick their puppy.

"Sir, other people are watching it, sir."

"No, they're not. They're trying to read."

"Sir, she'll take care of it, sir."

They looked ready to mace me as Cerberus aimed a remote and the sound bar dropped two notches. Still too loud, but I suspected the remote had a button for calling security, so I went back to inwardly-fuming docility.

The Diagnosis

When the doctor examined Andrew later, we learned our son's guess was right. "There's some elevation of the retina in the corner," he said. Surgery was scheduled for tomorrow.

The next morning, they allowed us to keep Andrew company through admission and prep. We met the surgeon for the first time, asked our feeble questions, and then it was time for our son to be wheeled away to pre-op.

From Janet's journal:

"Only one parent could accompany Andrew into the prepping area. I went. Hugh had to phone Arcadia, etc. A doctor started an IV. The surgeon wrote 'BH' over Andrew's right eye. I asked what that meant. 'Bernard Hurley, my name. We initial the eye that's to be operated on.'

They put a blue shower cap on Andrew just before wheeling him away. I looked into his eyes and thought that might be the last time he saw his mother's face, and I started to cry. He said, 'Don't cry, Mom.'

I hugged him tight, so he wouldn't see more tears, and told him I love him. They took him away from me, and I broke down completely, hot tears of self-pity and Godspeed-wishing and such a sense of sorrow for my little boy, who's been through so much pain. He is a Wednesday's child, indeed."

The family waiting room, 7th floor

Two men were sleeping in a deeply-settled posture that said they'd been there a while and still had a long ways to go. A woman knelt on the seat of a chair, facing the window, gazing moodily out and across the rooftops.

I felt bad for them. I hoped their person would be all right.

Jan and I were nervous. We started trying to suppress our cold panic by reading.

On cue, the woman came away from the window and used a remote to turn the high overhead TV on.

Loud. Static snow screen though.

The lady said, "How's this thing work"?

One man awoke and stood on the chair and turned dials till the picture appeared. Their voices were respectfully quiet, but why, if they knew to keep their voices down, did they let the TV yell so loud?

I'm thinking, "Geez, can't you folks live without noise from the world for a little while?" The occasion of medical danger calls for peace and contemplativeness. Consultants are paid lots of money to tell hospitals what colors to paint their rooms and what kind of art to put on the walls in order to calm people. Then they install these monstrous scream-boxes to upset us.

The other sleeping man stirred at the noise. I was just ready to say, "Excuse me folks, can we vote on this TV thing? Majority rules?" counting on the sleeper's vote, but then he stretched and stood and joined the others for a family conference in the doorway. The TV stayed on as a kind of bookmark. I gritted my teeth and tried to find a calm place in my heart. The woman stepped back in and remoted the TV off and left. Peace at last.

For how long?

I did not want to put up with any more TV.

I put my book down.

And walked into the corridor. No one there. Nor at the nurses' station. I walked back toward the lounge, trying to gauge the sight lines into the lounge. I couldn't see the TV till six feet from the entrance. Good.

Janet watched me come back in and walk to the end of the room and stand under the television, like I'd been sent to stand in the corner. She knows my proclivities, so she went back to her magazine. I looked up behind the TV, to see the hook-up. Two cables, a black and a white. I hoped they weren't screw-ons. They take more time than pull-offs.

The window lady suddenly appeared in the hall. I dropped an arm and massaged my neck. She stepped in and looked at me. Puzzlement crossed her face. Why would a grown man be standing in the corner, under the TV set, in a hospital waiting room, while his relative was getting his eye operated on?

I pointed at the landscape print on the opposite wall and said to Janet, tilting my head this way and that, getting perspective, "Yeah, you can really see how it works from here, the way the mountains blend with the sea."

The Remote Woman walked out.

This situation was ridiculous, I knew, and inappropriate. But I had felt assaulted, and my rights to worry in peace been disrespected. Yesterday, waiting for the diagnosis, there'd been that terrible TV in the waiting area. Now, during Andrew's operation, here was its nasty kid brother. And they were just two of the evil spawn of whatever coven had loosed them on the land. In my cardiologist's office two weeks ago, at 7:15 in the morning: The Morning Show. At the Social Security office on Midvale Avenue, while I sat captive, an intensely loud and violent video with Harrison Ford –The Fugitive?- split my skull. In nearly every restaurant that has a bar. In some supermarkets. Even at Conicelli Nissan, on Ridge Avenue, the small waiting-for-your-car-to-get-well room is dominated by a shouting 32-inch pain in the ear.

I waited under the TV as window woman walked away. Then I reached up and pulled the white cable out of the back of the TV. I left it propped to look like it was still on duty.

Twice while we waited, the three addicts came back for a fix but, "It's not working right," the woman said. When I was younger I'd enjoy a prankish scene like this. But today I felt a bit guilty. I wanted to admit I'd pulled the plug and then fix the problem, but I kept my mouth shut. Time dragged quietly by.

Post-Operative

Three hours later, the operation was over. We listened nervously to the surgeon. More extensive surgery than he'd anticipated. Everything looked good though. Retina was flat. Andrew came through fine. He'd awakened from the general anesthesia. He'd be up to his room soon. As for his studies—he'd not be able to read for about a month. Finishing the semester would probably not be possible. We'd worry about that later. More important, his vision was probably saved.

Jan and I waited in his room. In a while he was wheeled in. One of life's more horrible inducers of feeling helpless is the sight of your child on a gurney. Just as my heart sank, it rose again when the nurses asked

Andrew to lift himself onto the bed. He did. And moved to the middle when they asked him to adjust himself. When the nurses left, Jan and I stroked his brow, talked gently to him. Heard his kindly, polite voice respond. Oh happy day.

We sat together in his room, watching the shadows lengthen slowly across the city and along the wall of Andrew's room. A loving, still-a-bit-worried, family. Absorbing the peace from one another.

Just at dusk, I said goodbye and left. We'd talk later. I'd go down and cross the street and stand near the Wills Eye entrance, next to the bicycle rack, and wave up to the 7th floor. Bye Janet. Bye Andrew.

I left the room, feeling sad, but somewhat relieved. One critical stage of the ordeal had been endured. As I rounded the corner I could see some people were sitting in the family-waiting lounge across from the elevator. Some other poor souls still waiting to learn the fate of their loved one's vision. I pushed the button and stood with my back to the room. When the elevator bell dinged I stepped in and turned around and pushed the first-floor button. I looked across the corridor.

Oh no. The same people. The window woman, the guy with the key chain, and the sideburned guy, all still waiting for fate to make the call. And, to my chagrin, riding quite plainly at the surface of their worried faces was the easily-read disgust of people who are bored out of their doggone minds because … the damn TV's not workin'!

Darn. I felt bad for ruining their evening. I didn't need the lounge to be quiet any longer. Some people need television to get through their grief. I could cure that family's problem in a jif. I should just go in and reach up and slip that white cable back in place. Instant fix. I worked on the wording of my apology in my head: Didn't mean nothin'. Wasn't thinkin'. Not in my right mind, worried with worry.

The doors closed. I felt myself being delivered away.

Two days afterward, just so you know, the goo stuck in Andrew's eyelids washed away enough for him to declare that he could see. Just light and shapes, but after two days of total darkness, it felt like a miracle to us all.

The Sidewalks of Philadelphia

By Jim Harris

The old word on Philadelphia was that they rolled up the sidewalks at night. Well, nowadays they not only leave them unrolled, they cram them to the curb with trendy cafes and huddled masses yearning to be chic.

I don't know about you, but if I had to list my top ten favorite dining locations, pedestrian pathways in Center City Philadelphia would not be among them. Remember, this city was built in the 1700's, for tiny people who rode around on horses. The 300–year–old grid has not adapted well to skyscrapers and tractor-trailers. Dinner among the pigeons, car horns, screaming cell phone conversations, and toxic fumes of every ilk seems less than idyllic to me. Not to mention that there's barely enough room for people to get by.

I know that the theatrical "fourth wall" concept is supposed to be in effect. That is, the pedestrians are supposed to be invisible to the diners, and vice-versa, but sorry, Jim don't play that game. When I'm trying to negotiate a busy sidewalk, I am not at all averse to saying, "Hey, watch the fork, fella — you're in my no-fly zone," thus ruining the whole magical experience.

Okay, I admit, I am a little bitter due to a rather painful sidewalk-dining experience that I had recently. I was in the final stages of some very delicate negotiations with Japanese executives who were considering opening some of their "Sushi Queen" fish-flavored ice cream parlors here in the tri-state area.

I was eager to impress them with Philly's new hip, urbane image, so I took them to one of the most popular sidewalk cafes in town. No sooner had the waiter brought our hickory-smoked cheese wheel appetizer than a very hairy gentleman wearing only a "U.S. Mail" bag and one sandal appeared out of nowhere, grabbed the cheese wheel and took off, gnawing at it frantically as he ran.

Now I am not without concern for the hungry; I attended Live Aid,

Farm Aid, and a couple others I can't recall, but that goddam cheese wheel represented my personal piece of the American Pie, and I was not about to let it get away.

"Stop him!" I cried, but the fourth wall concept was in effect and no one responded. Outraged, I summoned the waiter, gave him a brief description of the thief ("… mailbag, one sandal"), and waited for him to organize a posse and initiate a hot pursuit, but he just stared at me as if I were speaking Latin.

Needless to say, I was mortified and humiliated in front of my guests. I briefly considered committing Hari-Kari to save face, but the only implement available was a short, dull cheese knife, and it would have taken too much painful, bloody work to reach a vital organ, so I decided to live with the shame.

And make no mistake, that's what we do here in Philadelphia. We have elevated living with shame to an art form second to none. Our sports teams, politicians and parochial ways may be the laughing stock of the civilized world, but we deftly stuff that all away and plod stoically along. We don't see any point in complaining, and we don't really care what the rest of the world thinks about us, or so we say.

One thing we do have here, however, is some excellent hospitals, and that's good, because if I ever catch that guy who stole my cheese wheel, that's where he's going to wind up.

Dinner

By Janet Gilmore

I told my boyfriend, Hugh, when we moved in together that I wasn't exactly the kind of person who has a full-course meal on the table every night. I'd lived alone for a long time and was used to "single woman dinner," which was often a can of soup eaten directly from the pot at the sink, followed by a couple of candy bars.

He looked at me.

He looked at my leather mini-skirt and said, "That's okay."

We got married.

I took my new responsibilities seriously for a time, but eventually reverted to myself. I meant what I said about being an inconstant dinner-maker; I'm not sure he meant "It's okay." Twenty-three years later, I'm still not sure.

I try. I go to the supermarket several times a week. Acme-land is a very scary place. Too many choices. My brain, which got me through college, a teaching career, and into Mensa, for crying out loud, stops cold when my clammy hands touch the shopping cart. I find myself in the aisles looking at shelves of potential ingredients, unable to put a whole meal together in my mind. The only aisle I do well in is the pet supply aisle, because we don't have a pet, so I can skip it.

Last week, I bought bananas, yogurt, milk and sponges. One of Hugh's mottoes is "Always buy new sponges," so I did. I bought an eggplant because it was a pretty color. Worn out by my exertions, I went home.

I called my friend, Edith, to ask what she was making for dinner. She's French. I thought, "I'll just do whatever she's doing and *voilà!*"

"What are you making for dinner?" I asked, after preliminaries.

"Stuffed eggplant."

"What are you stuffing it with?"

"Oh, this and that."

67

"That's a good idea. I think I will, too. *Merci beaucoup*," I said, hanging up.

Quelle coïncidence! I had an eggplant! I looked around for some "this and that."

We didn't have a lot of "this and that" in the house.

"What is dinner, anyway?" I cried out to the universe. The universe didn't answer, or answered inaudibly, or e-mailed me in invisible ink.

I checked Google.

"Google, help me out, here — what is dinner?"

Google did *not* specify meat, two vegetables and a starch all on the same plate at the same time with an accompanying salad, preceded by an appetizer and followed by coffee and dessert. Dinner is a meal, nothing more.

Meals satisfy hunger.

I can do that.

We had some leftover rice from last week's Chinese food, half an onion, a sad lemon with the rind peeled off, a lot of dryer lint, and now some sponges. I mixed the rice, onion, lemon juice and lint together thoroughly, baked them in the eggplant at 350°, and poured a can of tomato sauce on top. Cut the green sponge into small pieces and tried to pass it off as a vegetable.

I told Hugh I wasn't very hungry and I'd have some cereal later.

"This is awful! It tastes like dryer lint!" said Hugh, a man of sensitive palate. "Besides that, you *know* I could happily live the rest of my life without eggplant."

"At least it's a meal?" I offered.

"   "

"And it's ready on time?"

"   "

"Would you like some more?" I asked.

"   "

"Okay okay," I admitted. "You're right."

I heated up two cans of soup. We ate them standing at the sink directly from the pots, followed by candy bars.

Except for me.

I didn't bother with the soup.

Then I went to find that mini-skirt.

Finally Passing the Pregnancy Test

By Mike Todd

We'd been trying to get pregnant for almost exactly one year. Well, technically, my wife Kara had been trying to get pregnant, but I was pitching in as best I knew how.

As the months passed, I'd empty the trashcan in our bathroom and occasionally dump out a used pregnancy test or two, the disappointing results of which Kara had stopped reporting to me long ago. This is how it goes for people who actually want to have a baby. Teenagers can get pregnant just by sharing a sundae with the same spoon.

But just over three months ago, while I was deepening my crater on the couch playing video games, Kara came downstairs and held a pregnancy test in front of me. Sensing that the more important moment was transpiring off-screen, I paused the game.

"Does that line look blue to you?" she asked.

I stared at the plastic stick for a moment, and then looked up at Kara and replied using the same words I'd said to her so many times before: "I have absolutely no idea."

"I can't tell either," she said.

If you see one blue line, the test is negative. If a second line (the "money line") shows up, you're pregnant. But the instructions failed to explain what it means when you see one blue line, and then a few minutes later, a hint of a whiff of a line appears, one that is barely detectable, faintly grayish, perhaps sorta bluish and otherwise nearly invisible.

We decided that the worst thing to do would be to get too excited, only to face another letdown.

"The last one looked like this, too. I'll take another one in the morning," Kara said, heading back upstairs and leaving me to a moral dilemma: after the biggest news of your life may or may not have been delivered, how long should you wait before you unpause your game?

The next morning, the money line showed up slightly darker. By the following day, it was ocean blue, which was fitting, because we were headed to the beach.

After a year of trying to get pregnant, it has been our experience that the most effective way to get a bun in the oven, or, perhaps more fittingly for us, a pizza in the microwave, is to book an all-expenses-paid trip to Cancun, the kind that comes with all the booze you can drink. Two hours after Kara booked our trip, she came downstairs with the fateful pregnancy test that, in its own illegible way, let us know that for the next year or so, I'd be drinking for two.

In the few short months that Kara has been pregnant, we've learned so much. For instance, while a pregnant woman feels sick all the time, medicationwise, she gets sent back in time to maybe five years after we stopped treating people with leeches and whiskey. Pepto, aspirin, Ibuprofen and many other common drugs may be over-the-counter, but they're off the table.

A couple of days after we'd had the results of the home tests confirmed, I found myself in the pharmacy saying, "I need some headache medicine for my wife. She can't take Advil because she's pregnant."

It sounded so funny to say out loud that Kara was pregnant, like how the words "my fiancé," and then the words "my wife" used to sound so strange.

The whole thing was so new and exciting to me, I expected the pharmacist to wheel around and shout, "She's pregnant? She's pregnant! Hey everyone, this guy is a giver of life. It's a miracle!"

Instead, he said, "The Tylenol's over on Aisle 3, past the Q-tips."

The pharmacist's reaction to the news didn't give me nearly the lump in my throat that our parents' did.

In any event, something tells me that I'd better beat all my video games while I still have the time.

You can high-five Mike Todd at mikectodd@gmail.com.

A Knuckle Sandwich from Robert Mitchum

By Hugh Gilmore

The opposite of love is not hate, it's indifference. (Elie Wiesel)

Last night I wondered if I should leave the TV addicts alone. Stop prodding them, I thought. Be more accepting. After all, if I wrote about stamps, it wouldn't be fair to bray that coin collectors should join me in lusting for the "Inverted Jenny" or admiring the "British Guiana 1¢ magenta" or other such wonder stamps. Maybe even the toughest love won't get the remote controls out of the TV warriors' holsters. I should stick to helping readers find more good books to read. But how could I make the transition?

Perhaps the best way to shed the burden would be to step away from the lectern. I could pretend to clear my throat, or have a coughing fit, or even attempt one of my well-known, peanut-induced sneezing attacks. That would give the TV tribe time to slip out the back before we passed the collection plate for the Bookmobile. Or sang another round of "Leaning on the Everlasting Arms," like Robert Mitchum did in Night of the Hunter.

With the TV folks having slunk away, I could preach to the converted only. I'd adjust my string tie and look down at the faithful with Mitchum's sincerity. When the tension had grown tight enough, I'd lift my arms and show the backs of my hands: T-V-E-E tattooed on my left metacarpals, B-O-O-K on my rights. That'd be the choir's cue. They'd start humming Hing, Hang, Hung. And I'd begin preaching, belting out the one we'd all gathered by the river to hear: my adaptation of Preacher Harry Powell's Right Hand/Left Hand sermon.

"Ah, little lads, you're staring at my fingers. Would you like me to tell you the little story of right-hand/left-hand? The story of book and television?

T-V-E-E! It was with this left hand that old brother Cain struck the blow that laid his brother low.

B-O-O-K! You see these fingers, dear hearts? These fingers has veins that run straight to the soul of man. The right hand, friends, the hand of book. Now watch, and I'll show you the story of life.

Those fingers, dear hearts, is always a-warring and a-tugging, one agin t'other. Now watch 'em! Old brother left hand, left hand he's a fighting, and it looks like book's a goner.

But wait a minute!

Hot dog, books's a winning! Yessirree! It's book that's won, and old left hand television is down for the count!"

But no, that wouldn't be right would it? Aside from the obvious joy of being a goad, don't I have an obligation to raise up the least of our local flock? A rector's preach should exceed his gasp, or what's a column for? Let's say it: a book can change a life. No one ever said that about a TV show. Well, maybe a Powerball winner. Or someone living in a flood zone who saw an Eyewitness News Hysteria warning-banner crawl across the bottom of his screen during March Madness. The flood's a'comin', the score is tied. What to do? What to do?

The French Disease

What started me on that theme was this: I was watching The Princess and the Warrior yesterday, with Franka Potente (who played Lola in Run Lola Run), when her mental-patient boyfriend attacked and destroyed the common-room TV set. Everyone who'd set out to "have a nice day" was upset. After all, in hospitals, mental wards, prisons, auto-repair waiting rooms, bars and restaurants around the world, how are people going to "have a nice day" if a TV isn't shoved under their noses to tranquilize them? Naturally, the boyfriend who'd destroyed the TV was wrestled to the floor and heavily sedated. Soon after, the staff strapped him down good 'n' tight. Dangerous guy. In America, he'd be seen as threatening our constitution, at least the "ensure domestic tranquility" part. That notion of our forefathers has lost its original meaning. It now refers to the right to bear televisions in every household. It's a shared national prophylactic against the invasion of such French diseases as pensées.

Keep going, readers are the Bulwark against the insanity of Modern culture.

Stuff

By Jim Harris

"Imagine no possessions / I wonder if you can"

That's a lovely, lofty thought expressed by John Lennon in "Imagine," but let's face it, we humans need our stuff. We are the ultimate pack rats, running to and fro, buying, borrowing, and stealing stuff to add to our already overstocked stockpiles. You can tell how old a horse is by its teeth, or a tree by its rings, but a person's age is most accurately reflected by the amount of stuff that he or she has.

Communism and capitalism are both about stuff — who gets it and how much they can have. Buddhist monks have stuff. Even homeless people have stuff. They push it around in shopping carts as if it were a status symbol, and guess what — it is! In America — The Land of Stuff — you are defined by what you have. If you merely *drive* a fancy sports car, you are as venerated as if you had designed and built it yourself.

Whether rich or poor, we spend our lives acquiring stuff — so much that we have to rent space at public storage facilities to store the stuff that we can't stuff into our homes. Yet still we continue to hunt and gather. Junk men prowl the streets before dawn, scavenging the stuff that people throw out. Bric-a-brac freaks cruise the yard sale scene, often showing up before the announced starting time to get the best bargains. These "junkies" will haggle to shave a penny off the price of a thirty-cent item. It's all about the thrill of saving money, because money is also stuff that we love to accumulate.

The idea that one can save money by spending money has always seemed counterintuitive to me, but it is a basic tenet of Capitalism, trumpeted often and everywhere in such pronouncements as "Buy 12 doormats, get the 13th FREE at Doormat Town!" You can often see folks leaving those "big-lot" shopping clubs, straining under the weight of seventy–five rolls of toilet paper, in order to save forty-seven cents.

The key to saving money on a purchase like that is to live long enough to use it all. If you die with any left over, it might wind up in a yard sale, selling for mere pennies on the dollar, thus preventing your soul from achieving eternal rest. Speaking of dying, when you do die, try to do it in New Jersey, so you can save four dollars by not having to come back across the bridge into Pennsylvania. You can also gain an extra hour of daylight by dying during daylight savings time.

The most efficient method of saving money is, of course, stealing. Not only is it cheaper than paying for stuff, some folks find it both challenging and exhilarating. Even rich and famous people steal. The downside, however, is that time-consuming legal ramifications can result. I only steal when there is absolutely no chance of my getting caught. So far, my booty has been limited to towels and soap from hotels (I tell visitors to my home that my middle name is "Hilton"), and those plastic containers that carry the money through pneumatic tubes at drive-through banks. By the way, they make excellent containers for stuff.

Many serious accumulators of stuff will have one or two things that they covet to the point of it being an obsession. I have a friend who collects only rubber bands and upright pianos. Personally, I can never have enough duct tape. In our home, all of the pictures are hung with duct tape. No messy nails or wires are required. The only drawback is that the pictures occasionally fall off the walls.

Our garage is full of large slabs of Styrofoam that my wife cajoles from strangers at loading docks. She swears that someday she will actually find a use for them. It is also not uncommon for us to have three or four coffee tables at a time in our living room. We live with them for a while and then one-by-one eliminate the ones that don't seem to fit in. We call this process "The last coffee table standing."

Among our vast collection of old, useless stuff are such items as:

- 2000 non-working ballpoint pens
- 990 pointless pencils and no pencil sharpener
- 1 trampoline
- 1 very large blue exercise ball
- 5 dead computers
- 1.000,000 pieces of junk mail
- 7 televisions not equipped for DTV

Our credo is, "Save everything, throw nothing out." On the odd occasion when we do take something to the dump, we wind up bringing back more stuff than we took there. Occasionally we buy expensive new stuff that we never use. My wife insisted on getting a paper-shredder after seeing an Action News report about criminals rooting through people's trash to steal their identities. Even though I'm pretty sure that these trash-picking miscreants exist only in the imagination of TV news directors, we wound up getting a "Shredmaster 5000."

After a year passed and the towering piles of paper in our house continued to grow, I asked the wife why she was not using the shredder, to which she replied that she was "afraid of it." I understood. You see, we're pacifists, not comfortable around contraptions with whirring blades and such. Likewise, our hedge trimmer, power saw, and food processor, along with all 432 attachments, have been reassigned to "taking up space" duty.

I would have to say that World War II was probably the golden age of stuff. Back then, people were making and schlepping stuff — mostly weapons — at an unbelievable pace. In spite of all the unfortunate collateral death and destruction, war does have a way of making people very productive. Stuff is generally smaller and more sophisticated today, but we still manage to fill our lives to the brim and beyond with multitudinous magnitudes of glorious gadgets and gizmos.

To those of you who can truly live without any possessions, congratulations, you're halfway to Heaven. To everyone else, enjoy your stuff, and remember, maybe you can't take it with you, but you can keep it in storage just in case you come back.

Fever in the Mornin', Fever All through the Night

By Janet Gilmore

When I was sick and lay a-bed,
I had two pillows at my head,
And all my toys beside me lay,
To keep me happy all the day.

(Robert Louis Stevenson, *The Land of Counterpane*)

My life is usually so busy with one stupid mission of mercy after another, that I seldom get time to just lie down and relax for a nice breather.

Imagine my delight, then, when I woke up last Monday morning, after years of good health, with a *very* sore throat, a runny nose, and a prove-it 99.6° temperature. I was so happy – a day off! Stay in bed. Sleep while the sun shines. Drink hot toddies. Complain.

Then Hugh reminded me that, after months of trying to coordinate schedules, Plumber Jim Hanlon and Plumber Bob and the Giovannazo tile men were coming in fifteen minutes to tear the shower stall apart, replace the leaky shower pan and seal the whole thing back up again.

In my experience, several conditions must exist to enjoy a sickbed:

1. You can't be so sick you're actually miserable.

2. The sick-house must have a soothing, supportive atmosphere revolving entirely around your recuperation.

Our home, however, has only two bedrooms, one occupied by our college-age son, and ours, where I lay hoping for a long period of torpescence due to my illness. Unfortunately this bedroom must be walked through in order to enter the bathroom. I couldn't lie in bed in my favorite flannel, with lots of tissues and magazines, as working men walked back and forth through my sickroom. And I couldn't force the workers to walk through my son's room. So when the plumbers and the tile men arrived to start their work, there was nowhere for me to suffer but the living room sofa.

Where I lay, under a skuzzy blue blanket, with rolls of toilet paper nearby (the niceties of facial tissue long gone) and a near-filled wastebasket. Hair on end, no make-up. Books and a crossword puzzle on the coffee table, as if I could stay awake long enough to read or solve.

When workmen traipsed through at an early hour of the morning, I waved and held up the crossword puzzle, indicating that I was friendly, alert and able to focus — all lies. Temperature: 100.5°. I kept falling asleep, to be startled awake by tiles being hammered off the shower, the new metal pan being hammered into shape, and scratchy noises the tile workers made that sounded like giant mice.

The second day passed like the first, only I felt worse. Temperature: 101°. Still camped on the sofa with the same unsolved puzzle, but with fresh rolls of toilet paper. All anyone could actually detect on the sofa was a sneezing, coughing or snoring blanket, and a growing pile of used tissues. The lady of the manor was not at her best and not having any fun whatsoever.

No usable shower either, which didn't bother me, as I had no more sense of smell.

There is no such thing in our house as too much privacy. There is no spare room. I became a homeless person in my own living room, hunkering under a blanket and scaring people away. I had probably become one of the funny stories that Plumber Jim tells.

I was fascinated by how illness alters the balance of marital equilibrium for the better. The caregiver gives more than usual, and the sick person, however much she might long to do something useful, simply can't. The morally superior position, the goal of any relationship, is perfectly balanced for once.

"I'd better come keep you company," said Hugh, knowing perfectly well that I was watching a DVD of *House,* which he loathes.

"Great!" I croaked.

"You know how pathetic you are when you're by yourself – like a petunia in an onion field."

"Yes I am. Would you make me some oatmeal?" I asked, petunia-like.

"Of course."

Later: "That looks perfect!" I said, looking into the oatmeal pot.

"I'll cook it a little longer," he said.

"But I like it just like that!"

"No, you don't. Now just sit down at the table, Petunia," he said, getting a bowl.

There are probably as many ways of pouring milk and syrup on oatmeal as there are people with spoons on Earth. After 22 years of breakfasts, Hugh was about to make the mistake of creating a milk/syrup crater in the center of my cereal.

"No! No! No crater ... crater bad ... want moat!"

"What are you talking about? Is your fever up again?"

"100.8°. Moat!" I insisted hoarsely. "...Make my own inroads into oatmeal..."

"But that's not..."

It's *very* annoying when people do you a favor and insist on doing it their own way.

"I'M SICK AND NOT ENJOYING IT! I have 100.8° and I want MOAT!!"

He backed off, holding up the porridge spoon in self-defense.

I got my moat. It was delicious.

Next morning, my temperature was 99.5°

The morning after that, 97.8°.

The bad news was that my cold and lovely fever were gone.

The good news was that the shower was finished and looks great. Just in time. My sense of smell returned.

Not fair. Cold + fever should equal a lot more fun.

Janet Gilmore no longer lives on her sofa with Mr. Thermometer and Ms. Kleenex. She is now up and running frantically, as usual, from the market to the gym to the pharmacy to the library to the Post Office, to visit her mother, and occasionally, to the kitchen.

Being Pregnant is Not for the Faint of Stomach

By Mike Todd

Men who have never been married to a pregnant woman could be forgiven for assuming that the "YOU DID THIS TO ME!!" phase only runs for about the final ten minutes of a pregnancy, because this is what we have learned from our primary source of information on the subject, which is reruns of the show "Friends."

The most naïve men might even think that having a pregnant wife guarantees them a designated driver for nine months. This viewpoint is flawed for many reasons, not the least of which being that pregnant women don't need to go to parties to find reasons to spend their evenings with their heads in the toilet. They can do that just by sitting at home and waiting for a few minutes.

In the three months that my wife Kara has been pregnant, I've observed that the term "morning sickness" seems to be something of a misnomer. "All day sickness" or just "sickness" would explain the phenomenon much better.

I had always thought that the beginning of a pregnancy was the time when a new mother-to-be would stand in front of the mirror, lovingly rubbing her tummy and glowing while thinking about lullabies, tiny fingers and paint swatches for the nursery. Kara has certainly been glowing lately, but not quite in the hue I would have expected. The theme song of the first trimester appears to be much less "What a Wonderful World" and much more "It Ain't Easy Being Green."

Now that she's entering her second trimester, though, Kara is hoping for a reprieve from the worst of her symptoms. The stacks of literature she's read have promised better times ahead, if only temporarily. While there's no such thing as an average pregnancy, the general expectation seems to go something like this: About four months of extreme nausea and exhaustion, followed by four weeks where things are pretty cool, followed by four months where it looks like an oompa loompa's hot air balloon got stuck under your T-shirt, followed by many long hours of screaming, sweating and pain as the husband tries to figure out how to put the crib together.

In any event, most guys don't seem to understand, not that they ever entirely could, the difficulty that comes with carrying a baby, even before the most obvious stomach-stretching adversities have begun. Take, for instance, my friend Brian, who hasn't spent much time around pregnant women, and who inspired me to write this column as a public service to any men who might find themselves tempted to downplay the tribulations of the first trimester.

When he showed up at a mutual friend's house and found Kara lying down on the couch, taking up two seats, he asked if she could sit up straight so that he could sit down, too.

"Dude, I'm pregnant. Can't you pull a chair in from the dining room?" Kara asked.

Brian rolled his eyes and said, "Oh, I see. Playing the pregnancy card already."

I ducked behind the end table so as not to get caught in the blast that was about to knock Brian out of his Skechers.

"The pregnancy card? Seriously? YOU try being pregnant. I'm exhausted and sick all the time. Could you just drag in another chair? I need to lie down for a few more minutes," Kara said, hospitably allowing Brian one more strike than her husband usually gets.

Not sensing the imminent danger, Brian replied, "I mean, that might fly in the last three months, but you're like baaaaarely pregnant. It's not like I asked you to go clean the gutters, or handed you an axe and asked you to go chop wood in the backyard."

It was to Brian's great benefit that, indeed, nobody handed Kara an axe at that moment.

You can hide behind the end table with Mike Todd at mikectodd@gmail.com.

Honk If You Hate Noise Pollution

By Hugh Gilmore

Let us be silent, that we may hear the whispers of the gods. (Ralph Waldo Emerson)

A Confession

I'll start today with a simple confession and apology.

The confession is: March 13 marked the first anniversary of my purchasing an iPod.

Yes, me, myself, Mister Books. I bought an iPod. I've now owned it for one entire year. That is my confession. I'll offer the apology part after I finish the details of my confession.

Years ago, at an estate sale I bought several hundred blues CDs for a dollar each. Who could resist? I love blues. And this collection had everything from Muddy Waters to private labels recorded in church basements. I couldn't wait to hear them. But where would I listen to them?

Not at home. When I write, I need to think. When I read, I need silence. Perhaps when I worked in the yard, I thought. But no, this will sound funny, but I like to "hear" my yard. Any kind of recorded music would interfere with my ability to smell the soil and feel the sun on my neck and arms.

Okay, well then, yes, I could paint a room. Good idea, but a room would take, what, ten CDs tops. A second coat might help. Or a third. But, truth be told, I'd need to paint the Taj Mahal to get through all those CDs. The commute alone would exhaust me.

I owned a bookshop then. I moved the collection there. But I couldn't bring myself to play the blues during shop hours in a quiet, little, used bookshop. Too "branding." Too dramatic. And distracting. And people would ask, "How much you want for the blues CDs?" They'd be disappointed when I said, "Sorry, they're not for sale."

Well, then, I thought, I'll play them after shop hours. But that didn't work either. When shop hours were over, I went in the back room and wrote. Praise be to anyone who can write and listen to blues at the same time. I mean listen, not just type to the beat. I tried it. I can't do it. Not a word sticks, not a guitar line stays. I'm not a multi-tasker guy.

I put the CDs in boxes and hid them in my storage room. I figured all I needed was a second lifetime and I'd be home free.

One night at dinner I made the mistake of lamenting my dilemma and one of my dinner guests said,

"You should get an iPod."

"Fine and dandy," I said, "but when would I listen to it"?

"During one of your walks," he said.

"During one of my walks?"

"Yes, you're always out walking aren't you?"

Indeed, I was. Most days of the week, for at least an hour. Sometimes four or five. For a while I was practicing race walking with the idea of doing marathons. I could load up the iPod and listen to my blues tapes while I walked. Two birds, one stone. Double your pleasure, double your fun. Two mints in one.

But the headphones … Don't waste breath telling me about sound quality, they make me feel I've had skull implants. Help, there's a tiny blues band with great big amps stuck in my head. And the others, the ear-envelopers, create too big a sound for such a confined space— like listening through a stethoscope to a snowdome Village People's concert.

Too unnatural. But, since the alternative would be to pull a wagon with a boom box as I walk, I bought a little, mini, personal sound system.

That's my confession. I, nearly last, in nearly all, of life's competitions, broke down and bought an iPod Nano 4GB black. Sleek and light and thin enough to swallow if captured. I could load my blues CDs on it and still have room for granny's John McCormack records. And go out walking. And move to the beat. And, at last, my goodness, hear what I'd bought that day when I was offered such a bargain on all that great music. That's it. That's my confession.

And now my apology:

The darned thing's still in the box in my bedroom drawer. And the one-year warrantee has expired. Now I not only don't know what the music sounds like, I don't even know if the player works. Anyway, America, I'm sorry. I let the team down. But what the hey, it's my nickel. Was my nickel.

Daydreams

Usually I walk along our local Wissahickon Creek or on the track at a nearby high school. Here's what happens, either place: I've been indoors all day so far. I'm so tired of stale air and being cooped up that I feel like a big apartment-dwelling dog who's just been shown a leash. I can't wait to go.

I start walking, filled with life and air and promise and am grateful, truly grateful to be alive and able to propel myself. I say that because I have a ritual that starts every walk. I walk about a hundred steps and then I look into the distance and I say,

"Here's to you, Colin." That's my son, who died (age 18) one May day in 1988. And I picture his lovely face as I thump my heart.

"And you, John." My hometown (Colwyn) friend John O'Brien. Cancer, two years ago. He loved walking. He'd trade problems with me in a heartbeat.

"And you, Mom and Dad." Gently thump with both hands.

"And Aunt Anna and Uncle Freddy." Same.

"And Loretta and Mister Goodman." My sister, breast cancer. My beloved father-in-law.

"And Ray Pentzell." My friend and classmate at LaSalle, back when it was LaSalle College.

And then, remembering how people talked back where I came from, "The rest a yiz'll hafta take care a yerselves."

And, having remembered the dead, and having dedicated my walk to them, I am now free to look about as I float around the world. I love to look up into the trees from underneath as I pass by. It reminds me of the river scenes in Huckleberry Finn. And I round a curve and see other people walking and I watch them, wondering who they are and what their lives are like until I move my eyes away at the last second so they won't think I'm staring. Birds fly by. A breeze picks up. Buds appear at tree tips and then blooms come and the trees become so thick with leaves I can't see the birds calling from beneath the foliage. In the fall the leaves come down. I try to catch them. It's not easy. Eighteen is the most I ever found in my pocket when I did the count back home.

Then the snow and ice come and, eventually, spring again. So much to see, to breathe, different every day, an adventure every day.

My joints started to hurt too much when I was doing the race walk thing, so I've gone back to being what the competitive racers call, almost dismissively, a "health walker." Well, once a dropout, always a dropout I guess. I am healthier in the cardio-fitness sense, yes, but there's another kind of health that comes from walking like this.

I am alone with myself. I think. I remember. I try to see ahead. The synapses stop firing at their usual frantic pace. They slow down. Everything cools off. What a luxury.

In Your Ear

In case you're wondering, I don't play the radio in my car, either. Every silence is an opportunity. What a world we live in—there is always someone else trying to get *his* voice into *your* ear.

Commercials are everywhere, the great colluders of industry whispering, shouting, singing, banging, intruding constantly on your eyes, ears, taste, touch and smell to convince you to give them your money. We run this constant gantlet while we're out of the house and then, thinking we have escaped, we come home and invite them to assault us all over again when we turn on the television or radio.

And even when we try to escape via our headphones and music, we still face the prospect that we are giving over our ears to someone else's voice, someone else's views, someone else's philosophy of life.

It's a bit frightening to see the next few generations coming along, all wired for sound, but unprepared for silence. The sheer number of people who seem afraid of quietude staggers me.

And as for those blues CDs, I'll start listening to them any day now. I only have to choose to give up something else to make room in my life for them. Just what that shall be, or when, I'll have to decide during one of my walks.

Red Tape

By Jim Harris

Hey there, cowpokes, it's almost time to gather up those W2's, 1099's, statements and receipts, and start herding them into town for the big roundup at the IRS Corral. I'll probably be going to a reputable accountant this year, but my taxpaying past is full of shadows and fog.

Back in the 1970s, I used to go to a guy named Tony Ramshackle down by the Wayne Junction railroad yards. He literally had old tax forms taped all over the walls and ceiling of his dilapidated office, which I think was the only thing holding up the entire structure. I'd see him once a year for about ten minutes. Business consisted of a wink, a nod, and a payment in cash. The last I heard of him, he had left town one step ahead of the sheriff.

Then, in 1980, Ronald Reagan got himself elected president on a platform of getting big government out of people's lives. I agreed completely, so I stopped paying taxes. When the gravy train finally derailed in '92, and big government returned, the IRS sent me a rather cold letter asking where I'd been. I told them that I had been clinically depressed due to twelve years of Republican rule. They said that was too bad, but that unless I was legally insane, I still had to pay taxes, and that "By the way, you owe us a hundred thousand dollars."

On the advice of my old drinking buddy, "Eggy," I hired the law firm of Faste and Luce to proffer a deal for me. After several grueling rounds of golf — I mean negotiations — with the tax magistrates, they got my liability reduced. I agreed to pay it off at $100 per month for 75 years. The good news is I'll die before I pay it off. The bad news is Faste and Luce charged me more than they saved me.

Anyway, I just got so tired of dealing with anal-retentive "tax professionals," that last year I decided to take matters into my own hands. I bought a do-it-yourself tax-filing computer program. I popped it into my disk drive and a video began:

"Hello, I'm Harold Huffinstuff, president of Techno Tax. We hope that you…"

Enough of that. I clicked on first menu item:

Click …"Name?"

Click! … Income?"

Done!

The "Total Due" window then popped up, and said "$6,109." After blowing Snapple out of my nose, I went back to see if I had entered all my deductions properly. In the process, I inadvertently clicked on an "Amortization deduction" box, and I noticed that my "Total Due" dropped considerably. Now, I don't even know what "amortization" means, but I know that they should never have made it so easy for a lay person to manipulate one's "Total Due" in this manner. I believe that's called "entrapment." Whatever it's called, I was not strong enough to resist it. The last thing I remember, I was yelling "Ka-ching" over and over as I wildly clicked on the mouse.

The story picks up at my subsequent tax audit:

"Mr. Harris, do you own any oceangoing vessels?"

"No, not that I recall."

"Well then how do you explain this fifty-thousand-dollar deduction for the amortization of an oil tanker?"

"I, uh … that is, uh … "

I woke up in Chestnut Hill hospital with tubes up my nose, mumbling, "There's no place like home." A man sitting next to me identified himself as an IRS agent. He said that I had fainted and remained unconscious for two days, and that I was also under arrest.

I am presently applying to have myself declared legally insane. This involves filling out form LI-4F86, prostrating myself before a phalanx of government psychiatrists, and taking a series of multiple-choice Rorschach tests. Just in case, I am also applying for bankruptcy chapters one through thirteen, a grant from the John D. and Catherine T. MacArthur Foundation, and, if all else fails, political asylum in Afghanistan. I thought about Denmark, but everyone's so happy there, I'd never fit in.

Here in America, we continue to groan and strain under the oppressive weight of the most convoluted, jury-rigged tax system ever known to man. Like the venerable Ramshackle Tax Agency, it is held together only by paper and tape. Red tape.

Fontanel Follies of 1958

By Janet Gilmore

"While I was young I lived upon my mother's milk, as I could not eat grass... later my master gave me some oats... at this time I used to stand in the stable, and my coat was brushed every day till it shone..."

(Black Beauty: Autobiography of a Horse. Translated from the Original Equine by Anna Sewell)

I saw a copy of *Black Beauty* at the library the other day. Miss Smith, my 7th grade English teacher at Wagner Junior High School years ago, asked us, "Class, who wrote *Black Beauty?*"

Every hand but mine went up immediately. Miss Smith, of course, zeroed in on the one person whose little hands remained politely folded on her desk.

"Janet," she said, "You didn't raise your hand. Do you know who wrote Black Beauty?"

"The horse did," I answered.

I didn't really know. I had glanced quickly at the title page, then jumped right into the story. But I went ahead anyway, ignoring the feeble voice of common sense in my mind and galloping on to the literal, logical, simple-minded conclusion.

"Well, part of the title is *The Autobiography of a Horse.* So the horse must have written it," I said.

I don't know what I'm thinking sometimes until I hear myself say it, and even then my words don't always make sense. I knew my answer was impossible, but I was always blurting out the first thing that came into my mind. Laughing faces turned to look at me, *including Miss Smith's.* I was humiliated.

"Janet, what is wrong with you?" she asked in front of everyone. "I don't know, Miss Smith," I mumbled. "I don't really know."

I got some information though, that same year that gave me some insight into my "problem." My aunt sat my new baby cousin, Annie, in my lap. I was twelve years old. I touched her hand gently. She was so soft! I put my finger in her mouth. She sucked on it. I stroked her cheek, her chin, her little nose, put my finger in her ear.

When I touched her hair, I felt a soft spot on the top of her head. I ran my fingers over it, exploring, wondering. As usual, grown-ups came running from all directions, yelling, "JANET! STOP THAT!" I had no idea what to stop, or why.

"What'd I do now?" I asked.

"Janet, don't you EVER touch a baby's head! You don't want to hurt the baby, do you?" The speaker was a woman I knew well.

"No, Mom, of course not," I said.

My mother explained to me in her try-and-reason-with-the-savage voice that every little baby is born with a soft spot at the top of his or her head. The hole closes when the baby is about a year old, but touching a baby's head before that moment, is very, very dangerous.

I thought she meant that anyone could reach in through the hole and remove a piece of the baby's brain.

Yikes!

That was the moment I realized what my problem was! I reached up slowly. Yup, I could feel a small dent in the middle of my head that had a lot of give to it. And I knew suddenly and surely, that anyone could still reach into my head, through skin and hair, even though I was twelve years old, and catch a tiny piece of my brain under their fingernail and pull out some thought process that I needed.

"Yuck, what is this gray matter?" they'd ask, and flick it onto the sidewalk. Then millions of small brown ants would cluster around to eat it, someone's mother would come outside with a tea kettle and pour boiling water over the ants to kill them, and part of my half-eaten brain would be boiled and sent down the sewer with the dead ants to the Atlantic Ocean and I'd never be able to find it even if I could talk my parents into driving to Atlantic City, because I wasn't allowed out past the shallow end of the ocean.

Every time I did a cartwheel or a somersault, fell off my bike or walked into a wall, a piece of my brain might disject right through the hole in my head, I wouldn't realize it, and I'd never be able to figure out who wrote *Black Beauty*.

No wonder I didn't have such good manners. No wonder I was mean to my little sister. No wonder I said the first thing that came to mind, and thought that horses wrote books. No wonder my father sometimes looked at me as if I couldn't possibly be his real child.

THE FONTANEL IN MY HEAD WAS STILL OPEN! And in my family, intelligence was valued almost as much as pulling your hair back out of your face with a headband.

I quizzed my family at dinner, the night of English Class Humiliation Day.

"Do you know who wrote *Black Beauty*?"

"Anna Sewell," they answered in unison, even my little sister.

"I thought the horse wrote it," I said.

"Horses can't write books, Stupid," my sister said through a mouthful of pudding. My parents nodded in agreement and told her not to talk with food in her mouth.

"I guess not," I supposed.

I went to my room to double-check the title page. Sure enough, Anna Sewell was the author. I had seen her name on the title page, but it didn't quite register. I thought maybe she was the horse's trainer or another horse or something.

I vowed that evening to have the hole in my head repaired someday and to try to be more intelligent.

My husband mentioned the other night that *Black Beauty* has been re-printed in a new edition. He said the horse will be signing books at Borders on Saturday between 1:00 and 4:00. He thinks I should go. Maybe I will.

Wren Things Go Awry

By Mike Todd

When my buddy Derek recently opened our front door to leave after a weekend visit, a small brown bird shot into the house, flying right for my wife Kara like she was made of suet.

She saw the look on my face before she saw the bird.

"What's wrong?" she asked, followed immediately by, "Aaaaaah! Is that a bat? Is that a bat?" as she flung herself off the couch and scuttled across the floor.

The aptly named house wren alighted on the lampshade that had been just over Kara's head, then quickly made itself at home, conducting an impromptu self-guided tour of every lampshade and curtain rod in the house, mistaking each for a guest bathroom and returning the number of incontinent animals in our house to one. Apparently, housebreaking our puppy Memphis had thrown the universe out of balance. We were due for a correction.

As it turned out, Kara brought this upon us. The bird had built a nest in the wreath on our front door, and it wasn't even our Christmas wreath yet. Kara buys wreaths like rappers buy Cadillac Escalades.

"Oooh, this one would make a nice summer wreath," she'll say, pointing at an overpriced bundle of sticks and berries that will soon be riding home in our backseat.

Derek, Kara and I ran around the house picking up tools that we thought might be helpful for corralling the wren. Kara grabbed a blanket. Derek snagged a broom. After frantically scanning the pantry for a helpful bird-catching implement, I came back with the best thing I could find: an empty Honey Nut Cheerios box.

"Babe, a cereal box. Seriously?" Kara asked.

Unfortunately, I skimmed over the part of the Guy Handbook that explained how to remove flying animals from the house. It must have been right next to the chapter that explained why you'd ever want to change your own motor oil.

The three of us ran around the house, chasing the wren to a scene that should have been accompanied by Benny Hill music. I helped Kara toss the blanket at the bird a few times, but a moving target is really hard to hit with microfleece. In any event, if I'm ever forced to be a gladiator, remind me not to pick that throwable net as a weapon. If the blanket is any indication, I couldn't incapacitate the broad side of a barn with one of those things.

After several passes, Derek stuck the broom right into the wren's flight path, and the bird, dazed, flopped to floor. At that moment, Memphis, who had been altitudinally challenged enough not to have been an issue until just then, shot across the room, the thought bubble over her head clearly showing a rawhide chew with flapping wings.

"No, no, no!" we all screamed together as the bird hopped to its feet and ran towards the couch, with Memphis closing quickly behind.

With a head-first slide under the couch, the bird narrowly avoided the shared and shredded fate of every dog toy we've ever bought.

Moments later, with Memphis locked howling in the bedroom, Derek and Kara gently rocked the couch back as I crawled under with the cereal box.

"Hey!" I said.

"Did you catch it?" Kara asked.

"No, but did you know that the Honey Nut Cheerios bee is named 'Buzz'? I don't think I ever knew that."

As a team, we were eventually able to coax the bird into the box, perhaps due to the large print that promised lower cholesterol. Out on the deck, the bird hopped out of the box and flew into a nearby tree, where it probably swore off wreaths forever. If only I could get Kara to do the same.

You can smack Mike Todd with your broom at mikectodd@gmail.com.

The Spoiled Little Prince

By Hugh Gilmore

You may recall the acute case of "Reader's Stress" I suffered on a trip to Montreal this past June. I'd made the mistake of packing only one book for vacation, assuming I'd be able to buy more as I traipsed about. I read that one book the first night and then discovered that all the bookstores I searched carried only books written in French — which I don't read, speak or hear well. I writhed through withdrawal for the next four days, reduced to reading tourist brochures during the precious time I normally devoted to reading books. I was glad to get home.

A few weeks later we drove to Quebec. Like an addict who hides the substance he abuses in every corner of the woodshed, this time I stowed a dozen library books, all printed in English, in the trunk of my car. Thus did I insulate myself from further nothing-to-read stress syndrome.

What I did not insulate myself from, however, was the shame of being a "typical American" who cannot read the language of a country he visits. I determined to do something about it. Gosh darn it, I'd learn to read French. Maybe. At least a little — *un peu*, in French words.

I didn't want to take a course for several reasons. Even if I could part with the tuition without groaning, the course would do me no good unless I studied. But, my studying and memorizing days are over. Flash cards, verb tenses, masculine/feminine nouns. Just *dites non!*

I'd already failed the total immersion (TV-style) method of learning Spanish. Hours of watching telenovelas and "Sabado Gigante" had left with me nothing more than an ability to read aluminum storm window ads (mostly because the Spanish for "aluminum storm window" seems to be "aluminum storm window").

No, I'd try mastering French the way Hemingway did. I learned his method while listening to an audiotape on the way home from Quebec. On this tape actors narrated famous *New Yorker* magazine profiles from the past. I know that sounds like a parody of the sort of thing that the sort of guy that writes this sort of column would sort of enjoy, but it's true. On this tape Hemingway told Lillian Ross that he learned to read French by reading a story in *The Herald Tribune* in English and then reading the same story in the French papers.

I'd follow suit — in my own way. I'd begin with children's books and build my way up to Proust. I considered starting with the "Dick and Jane" readers, but felt confident I was past that. After all, I can say, *"Regardez, Richard, Regardez."* Or, *"Mon chat est 'Puff,' mon chien est 'Spot.'"*

But what?

Aha. In Quebec I'd bought a book by John Fante, a terrific American novelist of the 1930's (whose *Ask the Dust* was made into a Colin Farrell movie). The book, *Mon Chien Stupide* ("My Stupid Dog"), seemed interesting enough that I could wade through it with a dictionary until I bought the English language printing that would allow me to look back and forth till I understood.

Okay, reading time, book in my right hand, dictionary to the left. Also to the left, my wife — *ma femme*, I should say. As in, *cherchez la femme!* I believe. She too was reading.

Mr. and Mrs. North at home, after cracking several of life's mysteries during the day.

After a page-and-a-half of reading, which took a half hour and amounted to a description of a man driving home in a rain storm in a car whose windshield wipers didn't work well, I was feeling virtuous enough (and tired enough) to give up "My Stupid Dog" for the day.

That's when the trouble started.

I began to look for something else at bedside I could switch over to, something that would help with my count of books read for the year. But I noticed that my wife was reading *Le Petit Prince*. In French, of course. For the past year, at least half of the books she's read in the evening have been in French. I am, in turns, admiring, grateful and envious of her abilities, especially when traveling in French-speaking countries. *The Little Prince* seemed like a funny choice for her though when most of what she reads seems sophisticated, but there's never any understanding of *la mystique féminine, n'est-ce pas?*

"Would you mind if I read along with you?" I said, "It would improve my French."

"No, join in," she said, but quickly, in the way of someone who was caught up in a story and doesn't want the spell broken.

Well, I was good for about half a minute before I started putting my finger on a word and saying things like, "That means 'fox' doesn't it?" Or, "Does that mean 'sheep'"?

Within another few minutes I was reading the book out loud, in French, and doing that sort of half-translating/half-asking kind of commandeering of a foreign language book that drives competent people mad.

Only, *ma femme* did not get mad, she said, "I'm so close to the end of this book I want to go more quickly, so I'll read it aloud for you till I finish. And then we can come back and you can ask anything you want."

"*Okée*," I said with a hilarious French accent.

So, she read on. What could be better than to be Mr. & Mrs. North, in bed on a Saturday evening, my being read to by *une belle femme* in French? (Even though it was only a children's book, and a damned silly one at that, if you ask me, but what the hey, it was all so "*très*" something or other.)

As she read and the story moved onward, I noticed the terrific "voice acting" job she was doing. She brought great feeling to the story. I'd never heard her read so well. She made it seem as though she was terribly emotionally invested in this little story. Amazing.

But then, she came to a phrase she stumbled on. She picked up the dictionary, read the entry, tried several interpretations, seemed a little puzzled, and made the mistake of allowing a question mark to enter her tone of voice.

My cue to step in and straighten up this here French mess here. "Yes, it means venom, you know, snake venom. This is just before the snake bites him and he dies, you know?"

I was sure that would jog her memory from before, from when she'd read it before.

Only, she said, "He dies?" in a shattered tone of voice.

"Who, the little prince? Yes, he dies, don't you remember?"

I looked away from the page and saw her face. A moment ago she'd resembled the beatific Deneuve about to accept a kiss. Now she looked like the bereft Piaf drawing breath for a quavering shriek. Oh *merde*.

"The little prince dies?" she said.

"Uh, yeah, the snake bites him."

What is going on here? Surely she knows the plot is the same in French as it is in English. The prince dies in both languages. He dies in every language. Turkish, Chinese, Spanish ... unless, maybe, she's never read this book before.

"I never read this before," she said, tears in her eyes. "I can't believe he dies."

"He doesn't die," I said, trying to cover my blunder. "I just mistranslated."

"Oh that's terrible," she said, and began reading aloud again.

As she cried and read, read and cried, through the last ten pages I felt terrible. I gave away the plot. I ruined the book after she put so much work into getting to that point. What a jerk. I assumed my best, most sincerely apologetic body language and tone of voice and waited for time to remove the clouds I'd summoned.

In the meantime, the prince died on and on. The last dozen pages of that book have to be among the most maudlin, silly, tritely philosophic words ever committed to paper by a grown man in the entire history of literature on this planet. The prince's exit is worthy of a dozen Barrymores. I could barely manage to look contrite by the end.

Yes, in case I seem insensitive ("In *case*," he says!), I was sorry I spoiled the ending for *ma chère femme*, but she would have cried at the prince's death anyway, right? I just hastened matters a bit.

And where the ending of that book is concerned, I'm still with Oscar Wilde in thinking that anyone who can read Dickens' description of the death of Little Nell without laughing has a heart of stone.

It all just shows the troubles an American boy can get into when he starts reading outside his native tongue.

Dating Your Wife

By Jim Harris

Okay men, are you listening? Good, here's the scoop: Never, *ever*, under *any* circumstances should you agree to go on "a date" with your wife, no matter how much she begs you.

Somewhere along the line, women (probably single women with self-help books to sell) decided that "going on a date" with one's partner was a good way to keep some "spark" in a marriage, and the practice has spread like wildfire through the once peaceful, placid world of married life.

Please, don't fall for this trick. Remember, marriage is supposed to be your reward for surviving the whole dating ritual, and one of the great benefits of being married is that you don't *have* to date anymore. Dating is time-consuming, frightening, and often painful. On a date, you must look good, be charming, suppress almost all bodily functions, and generally dote on your date. Does that sound like the kind of pressure that you can handle? If not, then you will fail, and it is indeed a pass/fail situation. There are no shades of gray or honorable mentions.

As a result of interviewing over 100 victims of dates gone bad in preparation for my upcoming book, "Dates That Will Live In Infamy," I can offer the following lifesaving tips:

If you go to a diner after seeing a movie, find something nice to say about the movie, even if you slept through it entirely. "It was very sweet. I'm glad it all worked out in the end" is usually a safe statement. Be prepared to talk enthusiastically about clothes, home furnishings or yesterday's *Oprah*, and for God's sake, PAY ATTENTION!

If the diner has a TV, don't look at it, not even for a second, no matter how big the screen or good the game. Also — and this would seem to be a no-brainer, but unbelievably, men still fall victim to it — don't look at other women, no matter how skimpy their outfits or high-pitched their giggles, unless you want your head to be ripped off and placed on the dessert tray, right next to the lemon meringue pie, for all to see.

If you sense that you are failing the date, take deep breaths, try not to sweat, and keep repeating the phrase, "I am charming" to yourself (not out-loud). Be forewarned, men in this situation have occasionally gone completely catatonic and have even begun to self-mutilate. Women find this frightening. If your wife should run away in tears, do not panic, she's probably just in the rest room talking to a friend on her cell phone. Keep phoning her until she answers. Try texting the words "Honey, I'm sooo sorry" over and over.

If that doesn't work after half an hour or so, make sure she didn't take off in the car. If she did, pay your tab, call a cab and pick up some outrageously expensive flowers on the way home. There will still be days and weeks of meticulous rehashing to endure, and of course the failure will go on your permanent record, but at least you will have learned a valuable lesson — just say NO to post-marital dating.

Patiocity

By Janet Gilmore

"I can't believe that," said Alice.

"Can't you?" the Queen said in a pitying tone. "Try again: draw a long breath, and shut your eyes."

Alice laughed: "There's no use trying," she said; "one can't believe impossible things."

"I daresay you haven't had much practice," said the Queen. "When I was younger, I always did it for half an hour a day. Why, sometimes I've believed as many as six impossible things before breakfast."

(Lewis Carroll, *Alice in Wonderland*)

We are out of doors every year as soon as the weather allows, sitting on the deck, enjoying the fresh air, the flowers, and the birds in our small back yard.

Great food and great company increase the pleasure.

One recent fine evening, we entertained our friends Mary and Rachel with delivered Chinese food on the patio.

We watched the goldfinches flying in to our feeder and talked about the pleasures of being outside and the surprising variety of wildlife in our neighborhood. Someone mentioned the fearless, trashcan-raiding Chestnut Hill raccoons.

Rachel is a redhead with twinkly blue eyes and irresistible dimples. She adores animals, but doesn't suffer vermin gladly.

"Well," she sniffed. "We had raccoons in our yard on Allens Lane once upon a time. I know how to get rid of raccoons, but you have to listen and do exactly what I tell you."

"Tell," I begged.

"We had a raccoon living in the big tree in our yard," she began. "Her name was Sally."

At this point, if Mary smoked, she would have started chain

smoking. She rolled her eyes instead. She's heard this story so many times, she could tell it herself.

"Was Sally friendly?" I asked.

"She was fine until she had babies. Then she became very nasty and started raiding trashcans and knocking them over. All the neighbors were annoyed. I asked around, and the mailman told me exactly what to do."

"The mailman?" I asked.

"Yes, he was our mailman for a long time, and even though he was getting a bit forgetful, he was a very nice man and he told me what to do about the raccoons."

"What?" I asked.

"I'm getting to it," said Rachel.

"Do you have any white bread in the house?" the mailman asked Rachel.

"Of course," she replied.

"Take two slices of white bread and make a peanut butter sandwich," he said. "And cut the crusts off."

"Okay," said Rachel.

"Just a minute. There's more," said the mailman. "You have to cut the sandwich diagonally in quarters and wrap it neatly in waxed paper."

"Waxed paper? Not Saran Wrap or aluminum foil?" we interrupted.

"No, waxed paper. Raccoons don't like foil or Saran Wrap," Rachel continued. She leaned forward in her patio chair and animatedly acted out the process of cutting a sandwich in quarters and wrapping it carefully in imaginary waxed paper.

"One more thing," she added. "The mailman told me to put the wrapped sandwich in a small brown paper bag, fold the bag shut and put it on top of the trashcan on trash night. The raccoons will disappear."

Long pause.

Rachel filled the silence with, "Well, if the postman believed it, I thought I should believe it, too. He was a very good postman."

"You see what I put up with?" said Mary.

"Rachel, that is a ridiculous story," we said.

"Try it. It works. The raccoons never bothered us again," she said.

Mr. Gilmore scoffed, but I had to try it, following the cockamamie directions to the letter. Trash night was that very night.

Next morning, the sandwich and wrappings were gone, our trashcan was knocked over, the Hefty bag chewed through, and there were chewed morsels of waxed paper and brown paper, plus gnawed spare rib bones all over the ground.

"That Rachel," I muttered, as I cleaned up for the trashmen.

Rachel is 76 years old. She has told us about Rachel and the peanut butter sandwich at least ten times over the years. The story gets funnier and more preposterous every time. The harder we laugh, the more Rachel insists it works perfectly. If Rachel lives to be 100, we'll get to hear the story at least 24 more times, I hope.

Keep in mind: anyone who tells a story like that with total sincerity and such a pure desire to *help* should be loved, fed and protected on the patio. She should not be allowed to wander too far off, to where she might be carried away by folklore.

She probably doesn't realize that one of the things we love most about our patio evenings is *her*.

Janet Gilmore grew up in Philadelphia believing that woodland animals behaved like those in Disney cartoons, or were nailed to logs in dusty dioramas, like those at the Academy of Natural Sciences. She learned recently that neither is true: small creatures exist to feed bigger creatures and/or to annoy homeowners. Or both.

Will Mike Get Beaten Up for this Column?

By Mike Todd

While walking the dog a few weeks ago, I bumped into a neighbor whose wife was expecting twins any day. Walking the dog is a great way to meet neighbors. We've only had Memphis for a year, and already I'm on a first-name basis with Nicki, Brendan, Bailey, Lex, Misty and Trinity. For the most part, I have no idea who their corresponding humans are, but on this day, there was some chatting to go along with the posterior sniffing.

"I don't walk too far from the house anymore. And I keep my cell phone handy, just in case," the human said.

Once he discovered that I, too, had ditched a pregnant woman to create a moving obstruction in the street, he became interested to know if my wife Kara and I were still getting along as well as we had before passing our pregnancy test.

"Do you guys find yourselves getting into ridiculous arguments? My wife and I just had a fight about spoons," he said. "At least I think that's what it was about. There's no way to be sure."

Fortunately for us, Kara hasn't been experiencing the traditional pregnancy mood swings that we had been bracing for. It would be better described as a mood trapeze, really.

"Babe, I know you're not really mad at me," I tell her after she catches me putting bowls onto the "wrong" rack in the dishwasher. "It's just temporary insanity."

"It's not temporary insanity!" she says (insanely).

"You mean it's permanent?" I ask, horrified.

In all honesty, living with a pregnant woman is every bit as wonderful as living with the non-pregnant variety, and even though she'll try to blame it on the baby when she cries during an Adam Sandler movie, you'll remember that this is the same woman who cried during "X-Men 2" and the preview for "I Am Sam."

Kara is just hitting the halfway point of her pregnancy, where passersby might think she looks kind of pregnant, but will still generally exercise the good judgment not to say so out loud. If Kara were on the cover of US Magazine, the headline would read: "Does my wife Kara have a baby bump?" But then the article wouldn't tell you, because if a headline ends in a question mark, that means the author doesn't know, either.

The four-month mark seems to be the eye of the pregnancy storm, when Kara gets to feel normal again for a few weeks, though the previous months have been instructive about how it feels to go to sleep at 9pm, a bedtime I hadn't experienced since the 80s. Now that her exhaustion has gone into remission, we have settled back into our normal routine of me hassling her to stop reading and turn out the light.

"I'm almost to the end of the chapter," she says.

"How much more?" I ask. She flips five pages past her thumb.

"Five pages," she says, hoping that I haven't noticed her subterfuge.

"You know that I know that pages have writing on both sides, right?" I reply.

"Okay, ten pages. Will you scratch my back?" she asks. Now that her tummy is expanding and making her skin itchy, her back requires constant attention. It takes less back scratching to fill an Illinois Senate seat.

"I just stopped scratching your back twenty seconds ago. My fingers need a break. Ask me something else," I say.

"Will you rub my neck?" she asks.

Of course, I comply. While she's dealing with changes that make her skin feel like The Incredible Hulk's shirt, it's the least I can do. For the next several months, though, it's probably best if we avoid the topic of spoons altogether.

You can help Mike Todd load the dishwasher at mikectodd@gmail.com.

So Long Chumps, I'm Taking My Nigerian 419 Money and Hitting the Road!

By Hugh Gilmore

I'm not saying goodbye just yet, not exactly, because some details of my new venture haven't been finalized. But if this baby turns out like I hope, it's "Sayonara, Chestnut Hill, Hello Happiness!" I'll leave the area at once and go live with the rich.

I hope that doesn't sound snotty because I hope to retain the common touch despite the great fortune I'll soon have — as soon as my new business partner, K.W., transfers money to my onshore account.

I can't say exactly how many millions I'm expecting. I think K.W. isn't even sure, mostly because the international currency exchange rates vary so darned much. In another week though, I'll probably be able to absorb all the "wobble" the markets can dish out.

Don't get me wrong, I've enjoyed writing for the Local. But, as you probably guessed, I have the usual inferiority complex common to newspaper columnists — jealousy, at never having made "real" money. Soon I can afford to hire someone smart to write my column for me. I'll keep the byline, of course.

Until about a month ago, I had believed that my modestly abject lifestyle would always be limited by the amount of income I generated. What a chump.

Okay, I know you want some specifics. I'll start by admitting what everyone is thinking: Yes, I am lucky. Very lucky. Whew! Luckier than I ever imagined I'd ever be. But, hey, before we completely ascribe my good luck to luck, and luck alone, I will say there was some skill involved too. Well, okay, not skill exactly, but perseverance, preparedness, and perspicacity, the "3 Ps."

I was at the computer, putting in my hours, long and lonely bouts of time where it's just me against the world — me trying to make sense of it all, the world hurling its confoundments at me left and right.

Then one day an email appeared from Patrick K.W. Chan, Executive

Director and Chief Financial Officer of the Hang Seng Bank Limited, Hong Kong. My mail server, Yahoo, said it was "Junk," But I said, "Whoa, I'll be the judge of that."

I know you're not supposed to open these things, but sometimes … Don't you get the feeling people just say that to keep you from getting ahead? I opened it. Thus began a beautiful (and soon, lucrative) friendship.

Mr. Chan … Patrick … well, K.W. to me now —he calls me Gil — wrote to tell me he had a client at the bank who died with a big sum of money on deposit. And get this: the guy has no named next of kin and the expiration date for when the funds get turned over to the state is coming up.

Who was the guy? I shouldn't be a blabbermouth but, okay, I've gone this far I might as well confide a few more details. The guy was an Iraqi businessman and military figure, Colonel Hosam Hassan. A bomb hit his house. Took out him and all his known relatives.

How much money? 30,000,000 U.S. dollars. Enough to get your attention? It got mine. 30 Mil is serious money. That's basketball player money.

Okay, so I'm in. K.W. says, and I agree, why should it go to the city of Hong Kong? He can't stand that thought. Me too. So, what he's going to do is draw up next of kin papers and I'll sign them and present myself as the late departed Colonel Hassan's last living relative, "Hughy Hassan." K. W. says he'll draw it up so it's all legal. Okay, I said, just so's it's all legal. K. W. wants to split, him 60, me 40, which sounds fair, but I'm going to try to tweak him a little anyway. Otherwise he won't respect me.

We've got to work quick though. I Googled "Hosam Hassan" and found out that one of K. W.'s co-workers at Hang Seng bank, Peter P. C. Lee, is trying to swing the deal for himself (but only offering 65/30 with 5% for "expenses" (har har har).

And then, as if that wasn't pressure enough for K. W. and me, some yo-yo named Joseph Poon (from the same bank!) is trying to fool people with a similar next-of-kin offer for a, get this: "Colonel Muhannad al-Hakim," for $44,500,000 — an obviously phony, trumped-up name and number.

The one that's really got me and K. W. rattled, though, is Dr. Walter Lorna from the Taikoo Shing Branch of the London Bank Ltd.

He too is offering 30 million for Colonel Hassan's next of kin to step forward at his branch. Whoever does the Taikoo deal might go for a bifecta and run over to Hong Kong and try to take my inheritance while they're at it.

Okay, I'll admit it. I don't sleep that well at night lately, not like I did when all I wanted from life was to be a book columnist for the Chestnut Hill Local. But nothing ventured, nothing gained, right?

Besides, if this thing with K. W. doesn't work out, I've been opening a lot of emails lately that I'd previously closed my eyes to. How about these, huh?

Rowland Taylor of the Natwest Bank, London, is offering a Mr. John Yamnicky's $30,000,000 to someone who will show a little gumption and step forward as next of kin. His terms: 60/40.

Ibrahima Ahmed of the African Development Bank in Ouagadougou, Burkina Faso, is offering Mr. Lech Phillip's $15,800,000 for a next of kin claimer. Just starter money, I know, especially at the usual 60/40, but it could pay a .250 baseball hitter's salary for a year. Or buy most of the things offered in an issue of one of those Suburban Lifestyle magazines.

There are other offers out there. Johannesburg, Sierra Leone, Nigeria, to name a few, but, frankly, some of them sound fishy — and I'm not biting.

So … maybe you'll see me again, maybe you won't. Don't worry, I won't let the swinging door hit me on the way out. I'll be paying someone to hold it for me.

All names used were available by Googling as this piece went to press.

Dangerous

By Jim Harris

Recently, I was lying in bed on a Saturday night, watching an "Osmond Family Reunion" fund-raising special on PBS. As if that weren't pathetic enough, I was thinking, "Boy, these guys are good!" And when they showed old video from their 1970's TV show, I thought I detected a tiny tear of nostalgia trying to make its way out of my left eye.

Suddenly, a thought struck me like a thunderclap. Is this what my life has come down to — watching reruns of dancing Mormons in fringed vests on TV on a Saturday night? Am I the same rogue who used to arrive home as the neighbors were leaving for church on Sunday mornings? Is this the same guy who once woke up at high noon in a tuxedo on the beach at Atlantic City, amidst a crowd of little kids staring in wide-eyed wonder? "Mary, Johnny, get away from that man," their mother cried, "He's dangerous."

That was me — dangerous! Whether lying there on the beach like an unexploded torpedo, or jockeying for position at the Resorts Casino salad bar, I was a force to be reckoned with. Not someone you'd want to mess with, baby.

Here's an example of my once-formidable powers of retribution: In 1981, when I was the Philadelphia 76ers' mascot, "Big Shot," I got wind that the team's new director of operations, Lou Scheinfeld, was planning to fire me. Apparently he blamed the mascot's allegedly "crude" antics for the team's low attendance. I heard that he was going to make a big show of announcing my firing to the press, so I hatched a plot of my own.

I planned to put on my large furry outfit, alert the media, then go up to the 500-foot-high observation deck in City Hall tower. There, I would barricade myself in and strike a few poses for the press before hurling the big costume streetward. I figured it would play like a scene right out of King Kong, enshrine me in the "Insane Philadelphians" hall of fame, and bring well-deserved negative publicity to my front-office nemesis, all in one fell swoop.

In the end, I decided not to worsen my soon-to-be-unemployed situation by incurring fines or possible jail time. Instead, I sent Mr. Scheinfeld a publicity photo of a waving Big Shot with all but one of the fingers strategically erased. For good measure, I added a very brief (two-word) personal note.

I should note that in 2005, Philadelphia City Councilman Rick Mariano, who was under the threat of federal indictment, went to the top of the very same tower, indicating that he might jump off. He was subsequently talked down by then Mayor Street and police commissioner Johnson. It was about as exciting as an episode of "Dr. Phil." I think the councilman should have jumped — or at least put up a good fight.

Anyway, when I reached my 40's, I began to fantasize about having sons to protect me and my turf when I got too old to be dangerous anymore. In addition, they would carry on my legendary legacy of derring-do. I imagined three strapping boys — Adam, Hoss, and Little Joe — patrolling the borders of my sprawling Chestnut Hill estate while I rocked by a raging fire with my faithful hound at my side.

"Everything's secure on the perimeter, Paw."

"Thanks Adam, tell Hop Sing to start getting dinner ready."

It seemed like a dignified way for me to wend out my days.

That scenario didn't really pan out. I wound up living in a Germantown row house, sitting by a sputtering space-heater with my bald, three-legged cat on my lap, and the "Slomin's Shield" for protection.

When I go out in public today, little children no longer look on in wide-eyed wonder. I think most of them are carrying guns. Bravado has little meaning in a society composed entirely of lunatics. Life's no fun anymore. I've had to rethink my whole image. Actually, the Osmonds are looking better to me all the time.

Snow Wash

By Janet Gilmore

The first snow of the season was due to start at midnight. I knew because of the panic on the radio and television, and I could smell the approaching storm when I went outside.

Around 11:30, my husband Hugh looked out the bedroom window and said, "It's snowing already!" I jumped up to look. As I rushed to the window, he said, "Gosh, I hope the snow doesn't disappear by the time you get to the window." But it did! I didn't see any snow at all. How did he do that? It takes a powerful man to make all snow disappear in such a short time.

Although Hugh just might be the kind of man who would tell his wife it was snowing when it wasn't, just to see her run to the window in her underwear. Whatever his motive, I got back into bed and fell asleep, warm in the knowledge that snow was on its way.

Sometime in the middle of the night, Hugh came back up to our room from a successful snack hunt and I felt something cold and wet on my cheek. I opened one eye to see him leaning over me, a small handful of snow in his hand.

"Guess what?" he asked, quietly.

But it was not a real question, because I knew right away what happened. He had made me beautiful for another year.

"Ooooh, thank you…" I said, and fell back asleep.

Hugh was continuing a family tradition that I loved. My father snuck up on my mother for sixty years at the first snow and washed her face with a small handful "to make her beautiful" until the following winter. Then he did the same thing to my little sister and me.

He learned that peculiar custom from his mother-in-law, my grandmother. Grandmom washed faces with snow, too. It was something she brought from Latvia when she came to this country. She turned the custom over to her son-in-law, who carried on with great glee for the rest of his life.

I like being indoors at the first snow of the year. It's a very good excuse to stay in and do things that won't ever get done in benign weather. Tearing closets apart and putting them back together, dusting things and places that I usually ignore, baking, personal grooming projects. The day was fully scheduled in my mind by the time I finished breakfast.

I looked out the kitchen window as I did the dishes. Our street is a cul-de-sac and a hill. Our house is at the top, at the butt end. Snow always seems deeper here than in the rest of the neighborhood.

I went downstairs, booted up the computer and started a load of laundry. When I glanced out the basement window, I thought, with a jolt, about my mother at Walker City Retirement Home. My father was gone – who would wash her face with snow and keep her beautiful? Was she looking outside and wondering the same thing, or had she put it out of her mind, in trying to make an "adjustment" to her new home? Or had she forgotten all about it?

I tried to vacuum behind a few chairs, but my heart wasn't in it. I was worrying about my mother's face. And once the idea took hold, I couldn't get rid of it. No matter how sincerely I tried to clean.

I went upstairs and poured myself another cup of coffee. No milk left. I decided to brave certain death, or at least, terrible inconvenience, by driving to the store to get some.

The roads were fine, even our street. The overwrought weather forecasters were wrong – there was only an inch of snow. I made a wrong turn on my way to the market and found myself on the road to my mother's. I didn't turn back, because the mission pulled at my heart and car and there was no point in resisting. I meant to go that way all along.

I didn't phone before I went, because I didn't want to spoil the surprise, and I didn't know if my mother was in her apartment. It was just after lunch. I couldn't figure out exactly how to carry snow inside when I got to the Walker City parking lot. I needed a lot, in case she wasn't home and I had to go look for her. I took off my baseball cap and filled it with snow.

(*Knock, knock*)

"Mom, are you home?"

No answer. She wasn't. I'd have to go upstairs to the lobby and try to find her.

Now, Walker City is a giant building with lots of twisty hallways. I always get lost going from one part to another. If I see someone in the hallway, I usually ask if I'm headed in the right direction, but very often, they don't know, either. Everyone answers politely, and I set off in the direction in which I'm pointed, and I eventually get where I'm going.

This time, though, I had a tight schedule and a hat full of melting snow.

"Is this the way to the lobby?" I asked a woman.

"Yes," she said, and pointed. Was she right? She was.

The lobby was filled with clusters of white-haired people, sitting and talking. So many, in fact, that I thought even if I find my mother, I might not recognize her. She might look like an extra in a movie about an old age home.

So I walked quickly from group to group, looking. Someone asked me something, but I ignored him, because the melting snow started soaking through my hat onto the carpeting, and that could easily lead to committee meetings and new rules about carrying snow inside the building.

Very luckily, I spotted her sitting in a circle of her friends. She was so beautiful already; maybe this mission was in vain. She saw me, too.

"Jan! What are you doing here? How's the driving? Are the roads clear?"

"Well, Mom," I said, moving closer and kissing her, "The roads are fine, it's stopped snowing, but…" I took the last of the snow out of my hat and put it against her cheek. She was surprised, but she knew, too. Her friends gasped.

"Oh, it's okay," she explained to the gaspers. "It's a tradition in our family. To make us beautiful… my own mother told me to wash my face in the first snow of the year… my husband used to… surprised me every time… I never remembered…."

And all the ladies who had never met my father, relaxed, laughed and sighed.

I kissed my mother good-bye and left, keeping the mission clean. Beautify and go home. She was still telling the story to her friends as I walked away. I found my way back to the parking lot, put on my wet cap and drove home. I was certain that the magic would work. I don't know how my mother could be any more beautiful, but there's no point taking chances. You can't be too careful.

When I got home, Hugh said, "A cup of coffee would taste great about now! Is there any left?"

There was coffee, but I had forgotten to buy milk on my way home. It didn't matter as much as before, though. I saved my mother's face for another year and let her know that someone loved her, although it couldn't be my father. Just me, the daughter who forgot to buy milk and got lost constantly.

The one with a mission.

A Requiem for the Varmint

By Mike Todd

When our ferret Chopper first started having health problems just over a year ago, our veterinarian told us that the little guy probably had about six to twelve months left. I treated this estimate much like one received from MapQuest: a challenge to be bested, not an accurate gauge of the reality to come.

Chopper had already easily blown past the low end of the life expectancy range given to us at the pet store back in 2001, so we naturally figured that he'd just keep chugging along, munching peanut butter and sleeping in our crumpled sweatshirts until some point way off in an indeterminate future, some time when robots would serve us vitamin packs for dinner and the national interest in American Idol would have finally worn off.

It's difficult to grasp the peculiar charm of living with a weasel without trying it for yourself. After we taught Chopper to roll over for raisins, he quickly discovered on visits to my parents that Mom didn't cap his raisin salary. He'd walk up to her shoelaces and stare up until he had her attention, then roll over repeatedly until he got rewarded, which never took long. We'd become used to blankets and T-shirts on the floor randomly springing to life. Chopper had the uncanny ability to detect which jacket you'd need in an hour so that he could fall asleep in its sleeve.

I was anxious about looking after the little guy in the beginning; I'd never owned a pet before that didn't ultimately report to my folks. We settled into a comfortable groove after a while, though, and rarely has a walk been taken down the hall in the last seven years without a little carpet shark following close behind. Even in his old age, he'd hobble into the room to see what we were up to, then wait patiently until we wrapped him up in a blanket and set him down at our feet for another nap.

Some people have pets that could win a longevity contest against

113

a redwood tree. When we recently visited some of my wife Kara's old neighbors from back home, Kara did a double-take at a small gray bird that was hopping around and chirping in his cage in the living room.

"No way. Is that Petey?" Kara asked.

The neighbor replied, "It sure is. He's eleven years old now. He should live to be about sixty."

So Petey was eleven in people years, but in bird years he was really more like twelve. That bird will be in their family longer than their great-grandmother's armoire.

Unfortunately for our little family, Choppy didn't have the same Methuselah gene that Petey did, and our veterinarian's original estimate turned out to be only slightly pessimistic. Thirteen months after the original prognosis, we found ourselves back in his office last week, hoping that he'd recommend one more appointment but knowing that he wouldn't.

We consoled ourselves with the knowledge that it was the right thing to do and the right time to do it, and the whole event was peaceful enough to really be considered an anticlimax of sorts. Still, back out in the waiting room afterwards, I found it impossible to keep from breaking my personal rule of never crying in front a cashier unless there's a chance it might get me 10% off.

As we drove home in sniffling silence, I let go of Kara's hand to punch the radio on, making the obvious mistake of leaving the dial on the country station.

"What kinda gone are we talkin' 'bout here?" the man sang. "What kinda gone?"

I remember driving home as a teenager from our golden retriever's last visit to the vet's office as Creedence's "Have You Ever Seen the Rain?" played on the radio. Either radio stations somehow know when to play appropriately depressing music, or that's just what's always on and I only notice it after being traumatized. In any event, saying goodbye to a beloved pet at thirty turned out to be no easier than it had been at sixteen.

As Kara and I continued driving, the next country singer mournfully implored: "Fall, go on and fall apart," and we dutifully obliged. About halfway through the song, with tears flowing freely, we looked at each other, realized what was happening and simultaneously lunged for the power button.

"Okay, maybe no more country music for a little while," I said, which is probably sound advice under any circumstances. Kara blew her nose and nodded in agreement.

After a few days, we began to understand that we had just been through the final act of the best-case scenario for our pet. Three years and many fun times ago, I nearly flattened Chopper when he was hiding in a quilt on our couch, an event that I'm pretty sure disquieted us both equally, though he was quicker to forgive than I might have been. Fortunately for all of us, that day turned out to be chapter five instead of the epilogue. Eventually, though, even great books have to have an ending.

You can give Mike Todd a Kleenex at mikectodd@gmail.com.

ABOUT THE AUTHORS

HUGH GILMORE is a Philadelphia native who graduated from La Salle College and immediately went to work on a Highway Department sewer cleaning crew. He claims he must have inhaled something at the time because he's never been able to clear his head since.

Once, while doing his mannequin imitation he was discovered and hired to teach high school English, something every district that has known him later came to regret.

For a few mid-life years he was banished from the United States and lived on the island of St. Kitts in the Lesser Antilles, studying green monkeys, and later, in Kenya, where he studied olive baboons.

At the present time he is either happily, or inextricably, married, depending on who's asking.

The running title of Hugh's column is "The Enemies of Reading," only because his editor will not let him use "Free Will in Homo sapiens?" The column began as a sophisticated rant against all the things that get between us and our good intentions to improve our minds by reading more books. It has since then degenerated into a mere rant. However, occasional glimmerings of intelligence and passion shine through and Hugh has become an almost folkloric figure in the community, dragging behind him, wherever he goes, an albatross-shaped book. Hugh is an almost perennial favorite to win the least-heeded-prophet award given out each year by the National Television Association's Witless Council.

JIM HARRIS is a card-carrying baby boomer who has been writing since the age of 12, and has just recently begun to make sense. He has lived his whole life in Northwest Philadelphia, despite numerous attempts to escape. Among his many jobs, Jim has been a mailman, a singer/songwriter, and the official mascot of the Philadelphia 76ers.

According to Jim, "Writing a column is a lot like writing a song. The only difference is, you have to come up with a new one every week. I wish someone had told me that before I took the job." His column,

Hugh & Janet Gilmore, Jim Harris, and Mike Todd

"Life So Far" is a chronicle of events, real and imagined, in Jim's long, strange journey to perfect enlightenment. It is presently read by more people than the entire population of the island nation of Bom-Bom. He is also the author of the award-winning website, "Jimbob's Journal."

The minute this book went to press, JANET GILMORE went back to working on her autobiography called "Just Like Me," the story of a beautiful princess who had a nice childhood, grew up to marry the man of her dreams, had a baby, and never leaves her house, due to reality issues. You wouldn't think such a thing would happen to a nice girl who grew up in West Oak Lane, went to Girls' High, Penn State and N.Y.U. Her Master's at NYU was in Media Ecology. Halfway through the degree program, she asked her thesis advisor "Just what is Media Ecology anyway?" He replied, "Ah, Janet, it's whatever you want it to be." Since then, Janet's life has been a case study of that motto - meaningless except for chocolate pudding.

The idea for Janet's column hit when she read "Diary of a Provincial Lady" by Elizabeth Delafield. Janet tried to convince herself and everyone else that she was a genteel English woman living in the English countryside. She was even so deluded as to think she had poise and was capable of making quaint observations about the Post Office and the inhabitants of the village. What came out instead was a column about contemporary American manners. Occasionally some heart-felt sentiment is the basis for what she writes, but it almost always degenerates into balderdash. Janet's column is called "Notes from the Belfry."

MIKE TODD's humor columns won first-place Keystone Press Awards in 2006, 2008 and 2009. He was napping for most of 2007. Mike grew up in Chadds Ford, PA and attended Penn State for long enough to earn more degrees than he did. In 2005, he noticed a disturbing lack of journalistic effort to document his everyday life. His weekly columns have sought to rectify the situation ever since, helping his wife Kara to realize her potential as a boundless source of material. They haven't been married long enough for Kara to be described as long-suffering, but they're working on it.

Mike's column, "Over the Top," focuses on big and small moments in his life, from staring down the barrel of impending fatherhood to surviving his first encounter with scrapple. The Pennsylvania Newspaper Association noted that, "Todd has the literary timing of a stand-up comic. Writing humorous columns can be quite a challenge, but he seems to have an effortless talent for it."